I0011845

CCNP Enterprise (ENCOR) Exam Prep

350 Practice Questions

1st Edition

www.versatileread.com

Copyright © 2024 VERSAtile Reads. All rights reserved.
This material is protected by copyright, any infringement will be dealt with legal and punitive action. 1

Document Control

Proposal Name	:	CCNP Security (SCOR) Exam Prep: +400 Practice Questions
Document Edition	:	1st
Document Release Date	:	26th June 2024
Reference	:	ENCOR – 350-401
VR Product Code	:	20242202ENCOR

Copyright © 2024 VERSAtile Reads.

Registered in England and Wales

www.versatileread.com

All rights reserved. No part of this book may be reproduced or transmitted in any form or by any means, electronic or mechanical, including photocopying, recording, or by any information storage and retrieval system, without the written permission from VERSAtile Reads, except for the inclusion of brief quotations in a review.

Feedback:

If you have any comments regarding the quality of this book or otherwise alter it to better suit your needs, you can contact us through email at info@versatileread.com

Please make sure to include the book's title and ISBN in your message.

Copyright © 2024 VERSAtile Reads. All rights reserved.

This material is protected by copyright, any infringement will be dealt with legal and punitive action.

About the Contributors:

Nouman Ahmed Khan

AWS/Azure/GCP-Architect, CCDE, CCIEx5 (R&S, SP, Security, DC, Wireless), CISSP, CISA, CISM, CRISC, ISO27K-LA is a Solution Architect working with a global telecommunication provider. He works with enterprises, mega-projects, and service providers to help them select the best-fit technology solutions. He also works as a consultant to understand customer business processes and helps select an appropriate technology strategy to support business goals. He has more than eighteen years of experience working with global clients. One of his notable experiences was his tenure with a large managed security services provider, where he was responsible for managing the complete MSSP product portfolio. With his extensive knowledge and expertise in various areas of technology, including cloud computing, network infrastructure, security, and risk management, Nouman has become a trusted advisor for his clients.

Abubakar Saeed

Abubakar Saeed is a trailblazer in the realm of technology and innovation. With a rich professional journey spanning over twenty-nine years, Abubakar has seamlessly blended his expertise in engineering with his passion for transformative leadership. Starting humbly at the grassroots level, he has significantly contributed to pioneering the Internet in Pakistan and beyond. Abubakar's multifaceted experience encompasses managing, consulting, designing, and implementing projects, showcasing his versatility as a leader.

His exceptional skills shine in leading businesses, where he champions innovation and transformation. Abubakar stands as a testament to the power of visionary leadership, heading operations, solutions design, and integration. His emphasis on adhering to project timelines and exceeding customer expectations has set him apart as a great leader. With an unwavering commitment to adopting technology for operational simplicity and enhanced efficiency, Abubakar Saeed continues to inspire and drive change in the industry.

Copyright © 2024 VERSAtile Reads. All rights reserved.
This material is protected by copyright, any infringement will be dealt with legal and punitive action.

Dr. Fahad Abdali

Dr. Fahad Abdali is an esteemed leader with an outstanding twenty-year track record in managing diverse businesses. With a stellar educational background, including a bachelor's degree from the prestigious NED University of Engineers & Technology and a Ph.D. from the University of Karachi, Dr. Abdali epitomizes academic excellence and continuous professional growth.

Dr. Abdali's leadership journey is marked by his unwavering commitment to innovation and his astute understanding of industry dynamics. His ability to navigate intricate challenges has driven growth and nurtured organizational triumph. Driven by a passion for excellence, he stands as a beacon of inspiration within the business realm. With his remarkable leadership skills, Dr. Fahad Abdali continues to steer businesses toward unprecedented success, making him a true embodiment of a great leader.

Umaima Maqsood

Umaima Maqsood is a versatile professional with expertise in technical content development and proficiency across diverse domains, notably cloud computing. With a focus on Amazon Web Services (AWS) Cloud Practitioner, AWS Advanced Networking, and AWS Machine Learning, she brings a wealth of knowledge to her work. Detail-oriented and analytically driven, Umaima thrives in collaborative environments, demonstrating a commitment to delivering excellence.

Copyright © 2024 VERSAtile Reads. All rights reserved.

This material is protected by copyright, any infringement will be dealt with legal and punitive action. 4

VERSAtile Reads

Table of Contents

Copyright © 2024 VERSAtile Reads. All rights reserved.

This material is protected by copyright, any infringement will be dealt with legal and punitive action. 5

About CCNP Enterprise (ENCOR) Certification

Implementing Cisco Enterprise Network Core Technologies v1.0 (ENCOR 350-401)

Introduction

The Cisco Enterprise Network Core Technologies (ENCOR 350-401) v1.1 course provides you with the information and skills you will need to configure, troubleshoot, and manage enterprise wired and wireless networks. You will also learn how to use SD-Access and SD-WAN technologies to overlay network architecture and integrate security principles, automation, and programmability within an enterprise network.

This course will help you prepare for the 350-401 Implementing Cisco® Enterprise Network Core Technologies (ENCOR) exam, which is one of four new Cisco® certifications:

- CCNP® Enterprise
- CCIE® Enterprise Infrastructure
- CCIE Enterprise Wireless
- Cisco Certified Specialist – Enterprise Core

The ENCOR 350-401 exam, Implementing Cisco Enterprise Network Core Technologies v1.0, is a 120-minute core exam of the CCNP and CCIE Enterprise Certifications. This exam assesses a candidate's understanding of core enterprise networking technologies such as dual stack (IPv4 and IPv6) architecture, virtualization, infrastructure, network assurance, security, and automation. Implementing Cisco Enterprise Network Core Technologies is a course that might help applicants prepare for this examination.

Networking

Data exchange and transmission between nodes across a common media in an information system is known as computer networking. A private Wide Area Network (WAN) or the internet's Local Area Network (LAN) allows for

Copyright © 2024 VERSAtile Reads. All rights reserved.
This material is protected by copyright, any infringement will be dealt with legal and punitive action. 6

the connection of devices and endpoints (WAN). This function is essential for service providers, enterprises, and customers everywhere to share resources, use or supply services, and communicate. The Internet of Things (IoT), streaming video, and phone calls are all made simpler through networking.

Networking is a combination of a network's design, construction, and use, along with the operation, management, and maintenance of the network infrastructure, software, and policies. The skill level required to operate a network is directly related to its complexity. A large enterprise, for example, may have thousands of nodes and extensive security requirements, such as end-to-end encryption, prompting the supervision of specialized network administrators. In a nutshell, networking technology has revolutionized the world and created a new arena for the overall development of all regions.

Cisco Certifications

Cisco Systems, Inc. is a global technology leader specializing in networking and communications products and services. The company is probably well known for its business switching and routing products, which direct data, voice, and video traffic across networks around the globe.

Cisco certifications are widely recognized and valuable certifications that an IT infrastructure professional can acquire. Cisco certification training courses you will need to succeed, whether you are preparing for your CCNA, CCNP, CCIE, or CCENT exams.

Cisco's training and certification programs have been revamped to address today's dynamic technologies and to enable students, engineers, and software developers to succeed in the industry's most critical roles.

Copyright © 2024 VERSAtile Reads. All rights reserved.
This material is protected by copyright, any infringement will be dealt with legal and punitive action.

VERSAtile Reads

Cisco certifications

Technology	Entry	Associate	Professional	Expert
	Use this as a starting point if you're interested in a career as a networking professional	Master the essentials needed to launch a rewarding career as a networking professional and realize your potential with the latest technologies	Select a core technology track and a focused concentration exam to customize your professional-level certification	Become an expert in your field by earning the most prestigious certification in the technology industry.
Collaboration	CCT Collaboration		CCNP Collaboration	CCIE Collaboration
CyberOps		CyberOps Associate	CyberOps Professional	
Data Center	CCT Data Center		CCNP Data Center	CCIE Data Center
DevNet (Dev and Automation)		DevNet Associate	DevNet Professional	DevNet Expert
Design				CCDE
Enterprise	CCT Routing & Switching	CCNA	CCNP Enterprise	CCIE Enteprise Infrastructure CCIE Enterprise Wireless
Security			CCNP Security	CCIE Security
Service Provider			CCNP Service Provider	CCIE Service Provider

CCNP Enterprise (350-401 ENCOR) Certification

This intermediate Cisco CCNP Enterprise course prepares candidates to take the 350-401 ENCOR exam, which is the CCNP Enterprise certification's core exam. You must pass two exams to get the CCNP Enterprise certification: a

Copyright © 2024 VERSAtile Reads. All rights reserved.
This material is protected by copyright, any infringement will be dealt with legal and punitive action.

core exam and an enterprise concentration exam of your choice. And every exam in the CCNP Enterprise program earns an individual Specialist certification, so you get appreciated for your accomplishments along the way.

Following are the CCNP Enterprise Concentration exams:

Exam Code	Course Title
300-410 ENARSI	Implementing Cisco Enterprise Advanced Routing and Services
300-415 ENSDWI	Implementing Cisco SD-WAN Solutions (ENSDWI)
300-420 ENSLD	Designing Cisco Enterprise Networks (ENSLD)
300-425 ENWLSD	Designing Cisco Enterprise Wireless Networks (ENWLSD)
300-430 ENWLSI	Implementing Cisco Enterprise Wireless Networks (ENWLSI)
300-435 ENAUTO	Implementing Automation for Cisco Enterprise Solutions (ENAUI)

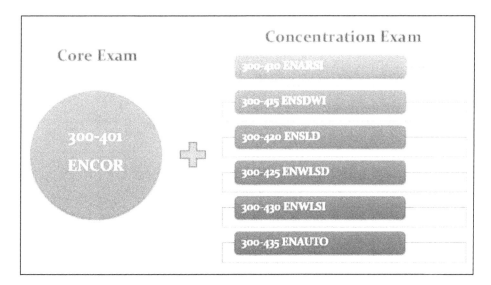

Why Can One Be a CCNP-Enterprise Certified?

Network management and administration at the enterprise level necessitate extensive training and experience. The CCNP Enterprise certification only requires one component, but it is the ability to establish, diagnose, and administer enterprise wired and wireless networks and their fundamental technologies. The first half of the certification exams and this training cover

Copyright © 2024 VERSAtile Reads. All rights reserved.
This material is protected by copyright, any infringement will be dealt with legal and punitive action.

the fundamentals of implementing and operating enterprise network core technologies before moving on to a more specialized aspect of enterprise networking. Because the CCNP denotes a high level of understanding of enterprise networks, this is done to demonstrate that the candidate has this level of understanding.

This Cisco course can be used as preparation for the 350-401 ENCOR exam, onboarding new network engineers, creating individual or group training plans, or as a Cisco reference tool for anyone who oversees network infrastructure training.

Who Should Take 350-401 ENCOR Training?

This CCNP Enterprise course is considered Cisco professional-level training, which implies it was created for network engineers. This routers and switches training course is for network engineers with three to five years of network infrastructure expertise.

Experienced Network Engineers: This course and the CCNP Enterprise certification exam are designed for network engineers with several years of experience. This CCNP Enterprise course covers all the essential technologies that must be mastered to design and maintain a Cisco enterprise network, which is substantially more complicated than most traditional networks.

New or Aspiring Network Engineers: If you are a fresh network engineer and already have a Cisco network certification, the CCNP is ideal. That will familiarize you with how enterprise networks are similar to and distinct from traditional networks and what you want to focus on in your enterprise networking career. You will master enterprise networking and set yourself up for career success with our CCNP Enterprise training.

How Does CCNP-ENCOR Help?

The CCNP-ENCOR certification is the required core exam for CCNP Enterprise certification, which help you boost your career in the following ways:

Copyright © 2024 VERSAtile Reads. All rights reserved.

This material is protected by copyright, any infringement will be dealt with legal and punitive action. 10

- Configure, troubleshoot and manage enterprise wired and wireless networks
- Implement security principles within an enterprise network
- Earn 64 Continuing Education credits toward recertification

How Challenging is the Cisco CCNP Enterprise Certification?

The CCNP Enterprise exam is challenging. Passing a detailed core exam and a specialized concentration exam, which can be even more challenging, is required to get the CCNP Enterprise. Cisco deliberately made the CCNP Enterprise difficult because managing and configuring an enterprise network is serious work, and they want businesses to be able to trust their administrators who earn the certification.

How Should One Prepare for the CCNP Enterprise Exam?

The first step in preparing for CCNP Enterprise is to decide which of the six concentration exams you will take. The second step in CCNP Enterprise preparation is learning, training, and practicing implementing and operating Cisco enterprise network core technologies. Finally, look for practical labs and specialized instruction for your chosen concentration exam.

What is the Cost of the Cisco CCNP Enterprise?

The Cisco CCNP Enterprise certification costs at least $700, although the core exam is a mere $400. There are two examinations for the Cisco CCNP Enterprise: the core exam costs $400, and each concentration exam costs $300, but you only need to take one. Although you can take one of the six concentration examinations, each one has to take the same Cisco CCNP Enterprise core exam.

Copyright © 2024 VERSAtile Reads. All rights reserved.
This material is protected by copyright, any infringement will be dealt with legal and punitive action.

Does Cisco CCNP Enterprise Expire?

Yes, like most IT certifications, Cisco's examinations have an expiration date, and the CCNP Enterprise is no exception. The CCNP Enterprise certificate expires three years after you pass it, giving you three years to either prepare for the new version of the CCNP Enterprise exam or advance to the CCIE.

Who Should Enroll?

- Mid-level network engineers
- Network administrators
- Network support technicians
- Help desk technicians

Prerequisites

Before attending this course, you should have the following knowledge and skills:

- Implementation of Enterprise LAN networks
- Understanding the fundamentals of enterprise routing and wireless connection is essential
- Understanding the fundamentals of Python scripting

Benefits of CCNP Enterprise Certification (ENCOR Exam)

Obtaining the CCNP Enterprise certification offers numerous advantages, including:

Enhanced Career Opportunities: CCNP Enterprise-certified professionals are highly sought after as organizations increasingly focus on advanced network solutions.

Industry Recognition: The CCNP Enterprise certification is globally recognized as a benchmark for enterprise networking expertise.

Copyright © 2024 VERSAtile Reads. All rights reserved.
This material is protected by copyright, any infringement will be dealt with legal and punitive action.

Skill Validation: The certification validates your skills in designing, implementing, and managing complex Cisco network solutions, ensuring you are equipped to handle diverse networking challenges.

Career Advancement: CCNP-certified professionals often experience promotions and salary increases due to their specialized skills and expertise.

Access to Exclusive Resources: Cisco provides access to exclusive resources, including training materials, communities, and events, to support CCNP-certified professionals in their career development.

Exam Information

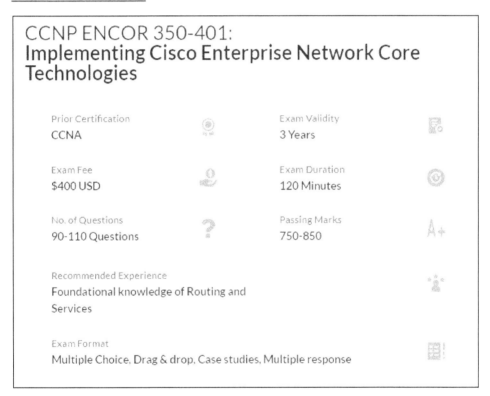

CCNP ENCOR 350-401:
Implementing Cisco Enterprise Network Core Technologies

Prior Certification	**Exam Validity**
CCNA	3 Years
Exam Fee	**Exam Duration**
$400 USD	120 Minutes
No. of Questions	**Passing Marks**
90-110 Questions	750-850

Recommended Experience
Foundational knowledge of Routing and Services

Exam Format
Multiple Choice, Drag & drop, Case studies, Multiple response

Copyright © 2024 VERSAtile Reads. All rights reserved.
This material is protected by copyright, any infringement will be dealt with legal and punitive action.

CCNP ENCOR Exam Preparation Pointers

Understand Exam Topics: Review the exam blueprint and study objectives provided by Cisco to understand the topics covered in the exam. Focus your study efforts on mastering these topics.

Utilize Official Study Materials: Use official Cisco study materials, such as textbooks, study guides, and practice exams, to supplement your learning. These materials align with the exam objectives and provide comprehensive coverage of exam topics.

Hands-on Practice: Gain practical experience with Cisco networking technologies by setting up lab environments and working through hands-on exercises. Practice configuring routers, switches, and other network devices to reinforce your understanding of key concepts.

Enroll in Training Courses: Consider enrolling in instructor-led training courses offered by Cisco or authorized training partners. These courses provide structured learning experiences led by experienced instructors and often include hands-on labs and interactive exercises.

Join Study Groups: Join online forums or study groups to connect with other CCNP candidates, share study resources, and discuss exam topics. Collaborating with peers can provide valuable insights and support during the exam preparation process.

Practice Time Management: Develop effective time management skills to ensure you can answer all questions within the allotted time during the exam. Practice taking timed practice exams to simulate the exam environment and improve your pacing.

Stay Updated: Stay informed about updates to exam content, study materials, and exam policies by regularly checking the Cisco Certification website and official Cisco forums. Be prepared to adjust your study plan accordingly based on any changes.

Copyright © 2024 VERSAtile Reads. All rights reserved.
This material is protected by copyright, any infringement will be dealt with legal and punitive action.

Job Opportunities with CCNP Enterprise Certifications

Earning a CCNP Enterprise certification opens up a wide range of job opportunities in the field of networking and IT infrastructure. As a highly respected certification, CCNP validates the skills and expertise required to plan, implement, verify, and troubleshoot complex network solutions.

Here are some of the job opportunities available to individuals with CCNP Enterprise certifications:

Network Engineer: Design, implement, and maintain computer networks for organizations. CCNP certification equips network engineers to handle advanced networking tasks such as configuring routers and switches, optimizing network performance, and troubleshooting network issues.

Network Administrator: Manage and maintain an organization's network infrastructure. CCNP-certified network administrators have the skills needed to oversee network operations, monitor network performance, and ensure network security.

Systems Engineer: Design and implement complex IT systems, including network infrastructure, servers, and storage solutions. CCNP certification prepares systems engineers to design and deploy robust network architectures.

Network Consultant: Provide expert advice and guidance to organizations looking to improve their network infrastructure. CCNP-certified consultants can assess existing networks, recommend optimization solutions, and assist with implementation and troubleshooting.

Security Engineer: Specialize in protecting organizations' networks and data from cyber threats. With a CCNP Security certification, security engineers have the skills required to implement and manage security solutions such as firewalls, VPNs, and intrusion detection systems.

Copyright © 2024 VERSAtile Reads. All rights reserved.

This material is protected by copyright, any infringement will be dealt with legal and punitive action.

Wireless Engineer: Design, deploy, and optimize wireless networks. With a CCNP Wireless certification, wireless engineers can configure and troubleshoot wireless networks, optimize network performance, and ensure security and compliance.

Cloud Engineer: Design, implement, and manage cloud-based solutions. With a CCNP Cloud certification, cloud engineers have the skills needed to integrate on-premises networks with cloud services, manage cloud resources, and ensure data security and compliance.

Data Center Engineer: Design and maintain data center infrastructure. With a CCNP Data Center certification, engineers can deploy and manage data center networks, optimize performance, and ensure high availability and reliability.

VoIP Engineer: Specialize in designing, implementing, and managing Voice over IP (VoIP) systems. With a CCNP Voice certification, VoIP engineers have the skills required to configure VoIP networks, troubleshoot call quality issues, and ensure reliable communication services.

IT Manager: Oversee the planning, implementation, and management of IT systems and infrastructure. With a CCNP certification, IT managers have the technical expertise needed to make informed decisions about network architecture, security, and performance optimization.

Demand for CCNP Certification in 2024

As we move further into the digital age, the demand for skilled IT professionals continues to rise, and certifications like Cisco Certified Network Professional (CCNP) remain highly sought after by employers. In 2024, the demand for CCNP-certified professionals is expected to remain strong, driven by several key factors:

Increasing Complexity of Networks: With the rapid evolution of technology, networks are becoming increasingly complex. Organizations require skilled professionals who can design, implement, and manage

Copyright © 2024 VERSAtile Reads. All rights reserved.

This material is protected by copyright, any infringement will be dealt with legal and punitive action. **16**

complex network infrastructures. CCNP certification validates the expertise needed to tackle these challenges effectively.

Growing Importance of Network Security: As cyber threats become more sophisticated, network security has become a top priority for organizations. CCNP Security certification equips professionals with the knowledge and skills to implement robust security measures and protect networks from cyber attacks.

Expansion of Cloud Computing: The adoption of cloud computing continues to grow, with many organizations migrating their IT infrastructure to cloud platforms like AWS, Azure, and Google Cloud. CCNP Cloud certification prepares professionals to design, deploy, and manage cloud-based networks.

Emergence of New Technologies: Technologies like 5G, Internet of Things (IoT), and artificial intelligence (AI) are reshaping the networking landscape. CCNP-certified professionals who stay updated with the latest advancements in technology are well-positioned to leverage these technologies.

Remote Workforce and Hybrid IT Environments: The shift towards remote work and hybrid IT environments has accelerated the demand for network professionals who can ensure seamless connectivity and collaboration across distributed networks. CCNP certification provides professionals with the skills to design and manage network infrastructures that support remote work and digital collaboration.

Industry Recognition and Validation: CCNP certification is widely recognized and respected in the IT industry. Employers value CCNP-certified professionals for their demonstrated expertise and commitment to excellence. As a result, CCNP certification remains a valuable asset for individuals looking to advance their careers in networking.

Copyright © 2024 VERSAtile Reads. All rights reserved.
This material is protected by copyright, any infringement will be dealt with legal and punitive action. 17

Practice Questions

1. At which layer of the OSI model do applications generate data?

A) Layer 1

B) Layer 3

C) Layer 5

D) Layer 7

2. What are the first Layer 2 network devices mentioned in the text?

A) Hubs

B) Bridges

C) Routers

D) Switches

3. Which OSI model layer handles addressing beneath the IP protocol stack?

A) Layer 1

B) Layer 2

C) Layer 3

D) Layer 4

4. What is the primary function of a network hub?

A) Reducing collision domains

B) Intelligent traffic routing

C) Operating at full duplex

D) Repeating traffic out of every port

Copyright © 2024 VERSAtile Reads. All rights reserved.
This material is protected by copyright, any infringement will be dealt with legal and punitive action. 18

5. What protocol does Ethernet use to ensure only one device talks at a time in a collision domain?

A) CSMA/CA

B) CSMA/CD

C) Token Ring

D) MPLS

6. What do network switches use to forward network traffic only to the destination switch port associated with the destination MAC?

A) MAC address table

B) IP address table

C) ARP table

D) DNS table

7. What does a MAC address consist of?

A) 16 bits

B) 24 bits

C) 32 bits

D) 48 bits

8. Which MAC address is reserved for network broadcasts?

A) 00:00:00:00:00:00

B) FF:FF:FF:FF:FF

C) 11:11:11:11:11:11

D) AA:AA:AA:AA:AA

Copyright © 2024 VERSAtile Reads. All rights reserved.

This material is protected by copyright, any infringement will be dealt with legal and punitive action.

9. What technology is used to create multiple broadcast domains on the same network switch?

A) VLANs

B) VPNs

C) VTP

D) VRRP

10. Which IEEE standard defines VLANs?

A) 802.11

B) 802.1Q

C) 802.3

D) 802.16

11. How many bits are allocated to the VLAN identifier in the 802.1Q standard?

A) 8 bits

B) 10 bits

C) 12 bits

D) 16 bits

12. Which VLAN is reserved for 802.1P traffic and cannot be modified or deleted?

A) VLAN 0

B) VLAN 1

C) VLAN 1001

D) VLAN 4094

Copyright © 2024 VERSAtile Reads. All rights reserved.

This material is protected by copyright, any infringement will be dealt with legal and punitive action. 20

13. What is the default VLAN on Catalyst switches?

A) VLAN 0

B) VLAN 1

C) VLAN 1001

D) VLAN 4094

14. What type of port is assigned to only one VLAN and carries traffic from that VLAN to the connected device?

A) Trunk port

B) Access port

C) Virtual port

D) Broadcast port

15. What command is used to configure a port as an access port manually?

A) switchport mode access

B) switchport mode trunk

C) switchport mode dynamic

D) switchport mode hybrid

16. Trunk ports can carry traffic for how many VLANs?

A) One

B) Two

C) Multiple

D) None

17. Which command is used to specify which VLANs are allowed to traverse a trunk port?

Copyright © 2024 VERSAtile Reads. All rights reserved.

This material is protected by copyright, any infringement will be dealt with legal and punitive action. 21

VERSAtile Reads

A) switchport trunk allowed vlan

B) switchport access vlan

C) switchport native vlan

D) switchport vlan

18. What is the default native VLAN on trunk ports?

A) VLAN 1

B) VLAN 10

C) VLAN 1001

D) VLAN 4094

19. What is the primary purpose of the native VLAN?

A) Carry user data

B) Prevent broadcast storms

C) Advertise switch control traffic

D) Handle untagged traffic

20. Which command syntax is used to add VLANs to those already listed on a trunk port?

A) switchport trunk allowed vlan vlan-ids

B) switchport trunk allowed add vlan-ids

C) switchport trunk allowed remove vlan-ids

D) switchport trunk allowed except vlan-ids

21. What diagnostic command provides information about trunk ports, including associated VLANs and status?

A) show interfaces

Copyright © 2024 VERSAtile Reads. All rights reserved.

This material is protected by copyright, any infringement will be dealt with legal and punitive action. 22

B) show vlan

C) show spanning-tree

D) show interfaces trunk

22. Which section of the output of the show interfaces trunk command displays the list of VLANs allowed on the trunk port?

A) Section 1

B) Section 2

C) Section 3

D) Section 4

23. What type of traffic is associated with the native VLAN on trunk ports?

A) Broadcast

B) Management

C) User data

D) Control

24. Which of the following is NOT a benefit of using VLANs?

A) Higher utilization of switch ports

B) Reduced broadcast domains

C) Improved network security

D) Increased collision domains

25. Which of the following EIGRP configuration commands allows the advertisement of a default route?

A) default-information originate

B) redistribute static

Copyright © 2024 VERSAtile Reads. All rights reserved.

This material is protected by copyright, any infringement will be dealt with legal and punitive action. 23

C) ip default-network

D) network 0.0.0.0

26. What does CSMA/CD stand for?

A) Carrier Sense Multiple Access/Carrier Detect

B) Carrier Sense Multiple Access/Collision Detect

C) Collision Sensing Multiple Access/Carrier Detect

D) Collision Sensing Multiple Access/Collision Detect

27. What is the purpose of CSMA/CD in Ethernet networks?

A) To prevent collisions

B) To detect errors in transmission

C) To manage network traffic

D) To ensure secure communication

28. What protocol is commonly used for Layer 2 addressing in Ethernet networks?

A) IP

B) MAC

C) TCP

D) UDP

29. How does a switch forward network traffic?

A) Based on IP addresses

B) Based on MAC addresses

C) Based on port numbers

Copyright © 2024 VERSAtile Reads. All rights reserved.

This material is protected by copyright, any infringement will be dealt with legal and punitive action.

D) Based on subnet masks

30. What is the primary function of a network bridge?

A) Segmenting broadcast domains

B) Filtering traffic based on VLANs

C) Forwarding traffic based on IP addresses

D) Repeating traffic out of every port

31. Which of the following is a characteristic of Layer 2 switches?

A) Operate at the application layer

B) Use IP addresses for forwarding decisions

C) Forward traffic based on MAC addresses

D) Route traffic between different networks

32. What type of network device operates at the data link layer (Layer 2) of the OSI model?

A) Router

B) Switch

C) Firewall

D) Server

33. Which networking device is primarily responsible for determining the best path for data packets to reach their destination?

A) Hub

B) Bridge

C) Router

D) Switch

Copyright © 2024 VERSAtile Reads. All rights reserved.

This material is protected by copyright, any infringement will be dealt with legal and punitive action.

34. Which OSI layer is responsible for establishing, maintaining, and terminating connections between applications?

A) Presentation layer

B) Transport layer

C) Session layer

D) Application layer

35. Which protocol operates at the network layer (Layer 3) of the OSI model?

A) HTTP

B) FTP

C) TCP

D) IP

36. What is the primary function of the network layer (Layer 3) in the OSI model?

A) Provides encryption for data transmission

B) Transmits data between adjacent network nodes

C) Defines the physical characteristics of the network medium

D) Routes data packets to their destinations

37. What does TCP stand for?

A) Transmission Control Protocol

B) Transfer Control Protocol

C) Transport Control Protocol

D) Technical Control Protocol

Copyright © 2024 VERSAtile Reads. All rights reserved.
This material is protected by copyright, any infringement will be dealt with legal and punitive action.

VERSAtile Reads

38. Which transport layer protocol provides reliable, connection-oriented communication between devices?

A) UDP

B) IP

C) TCP

D) ICMP

39. In which layer of the OSI model do switches operate?

A) Network layer (Layer 3)

B) Data link layer (Layer 2)

C) Transport layer (Layer 4)

D) Application layer (Layer 7)

40. What is the purpose of the Data Link layer in the OSI model?

A) Ensures reliable end-to-end data transmission

B) Manages data traffic between nodes on a network

C) Translates data into a format suitable for transmission over the network

D) Provides error detection and correction mechanisms

41. What is the function of the Transport layer in the OSI model?

A) Handles the physical transmission of data over the network medium

B) Establishes, maintains, and terminates connections between network nodes

C) Manages data traffic between applications running on different hosts

D) Routes data packets to their destination based on logical addressing

Copyright © 2024 VERSAtile Reads. All rights reserved.
This material is protected by copyright, any infringement will be dealt with legal and punitive action. 27

42. What is the role of the Presentation layer in the OSI model?

A) Provides encryption and decryption services for secure data transmission

B) Format data for presentation to the user

C) Manages the flow of data between devices on the network

D) Ensures reliable end-to-end delivery of data packets

43. Which layer of the OSI model is responsible for converting data into a format suitable for transmission over the network?

A) Network layer

B) Transport layer

C) Data Link layer

D) Presentation layer

44. What is the primary function of the Application layer in the OSI model?

A) Establishes, maintains, and terminates connections between network nodes

B) Provides encryption and decryption services for secure data transmission

C) Manages data traffic between applications running on different hosts

D) Allows access to network services for user applications

45. Which of the following is NOT a characteristic of the OSI model?

A) It provides a standard framework for understanding and designing network protocols.

B) It consists of seven layers, each with a specific function.

C) It is a proprietary model developed by Cisco Systems.

Copyright © 2024 VERSAtile Reads. All rights reserved.
This material is protected by copyright, any infringement will be dealt with legal and punitive action.

D) It allows different vendors to create interoperable networking devices and software.

46. What is the primary benefit of using a layered approach like the OSI model in networking?

A) It simplifies the design and implementation of complex networking systems.

B) It ensures that all networking devices and software are compatible with each other.

C) It provides a standard framework for troubleshooting network issues.

D) It increases network performance and efficiency.

47. Which layer of the OSI model is responsible for error detection and recovery?

A) Data Link layer

B) Transport layer

C) Network layer

D) Presentation layer

48. Which OSI layer is responsible for logical addressing and routing?

A) Data Link layer

B) Network layer

C) Transport layer

D) Session layer

49. Which layer of the OSI model provides a common interface for applications to access network services?

A) Presentation layer

Copyright © 2024 VERSAtile Reads. All rights reserved.
This material is protected by copyright, any infringement will be dealt with legal and punitive action.

B) Session layer

C) Transport layer

D) Application layer

50. What is the purpose of having a static MAC address entry in the MAC address table?

A) To facilitate unknown unicast flooding

B) To prevent unknown unicast flooding

C) To facilitate unknown multicast flooding

D) To prevent unknown multicast flooding

51. Which command adds a manual entry to the MAC address table with the ability to associate it to a specific switch port or to drop traffic upon receipt?

A) mac address-table static

B) mac address-table dynamic

C) show interfaces switchport

D) clear mac address-table dynamic

52. What type of memory does the MAC address table reside in?

A) Random Access Memory (RAM)

B) Read-Only Memory (ROM)

C) Content Addressable Memory (CAM)

D) Flash Memory

53. How does the CAM provide results for any query?

A) By providing a decimal result

Copyright © 2024 VERSAtile Reads. All rights reserved.
This material is protected by copyright, any infringement will be dealt with legal and punitive action.

B) By providing a hexadecimal result

C) By providing a binary result

D) By providing an ASCII result

54. Which command can be used to flush the MAC address table for the entire switch?

A) mac address-table static

B) show interfaces switchport

C) clear mac address-table dynamic

D) show interface status

55. What information does the command "show interfaces interface-id switchport" provide?

A) Overall interface status

B) Switch port status

C) Layer 3 forwarding details

D) MAC address table details

56. What is the operational mode of port Gi1/0/5?

A) Up

B) Down

C) Auto

D) Trunk

57. Which field in the "show interface status" command indicates whether a link is connected or not?

A) Port

Copyright © 2024 VERSAtile Reads. All rights reserved.

This material is protected by copyright, any infringement will be dealt with legal and punitive action.

B) Name

C) Status

D) VLAN

58. How are trunk links represented in the "show interface status" output?

A) As connected

B) As notconnect

C) As trunk

D) As routed

59. What is the purpose of the ARP table?

A) To map Layer 3 IP addresses to Layer 4 port numbers

B) To map Layer 3 IP addresses to Layer 2 MAC addresses

C) To map Layer 2 MAC addresses to Layer 1 physical addresses

D) To map Layer 2 MAC addresses to Layer 3 IP addresses

60. How does a device update its local ARP table upon receipt of an ARP reply?

A) By broadcasting an ARP request

B) By sending a unicast response

C) By adding Layer 2 headers

D) By flushing the ARP cache

61. When must packets be routed?

A) When devices are on the same network

B) When devices are on different networks

Copyright © 2024 VERSAtile Reads. All rights reserved.
This material is protected by copyright, any infringement will be dealt with legal and punitive action. 32

C) When devices are on the same subnet

D) When devices are on different subnets

62. What is the purpose of the source device checking its local routing table?

A) To identify its next-hop IP address

B) To identify its own IP address

C) To identify its subnet mask

D) To identify its MAC address

63. Which entry in the routing table is learned from a default gateway?

A) Connected routes

B) Static routes

C) Dynamic routes

D) Floating routes

64. What information is needed by the source device to forward packets to a different network?

A) Source IP address

B) Destination IP address

C) Source MAC address

D) Destination MAC address

65. In the process of packet routing, what does the next router modify in the packet?

A) Source IP address

B) Destination IP address

Copyright © 2024 VERSAtile Reads. All rights reserved.
This material is protected by copyright, any infringement will be dealt with legal and punitive action.

C) Source MAC address

D) Destination MAC address

66. What does the concept of Layer 2 addressing rewrite involve?

A) Changing IP addresses

B) Changing MAC addresses

C) Changing subnet masks

D) Changing VLAN IDs

67. Which command can be used to view the ARP table?

A) show ip arp

B) show mac-address-table

C) show interfaces switchport

D) show interface status

68. What is the purpose of adding a secondary IPv4 address to an interface?

A) To create a redundant connection

B) To increase the interface speed

C) To allow multiple IPv4 networks on the same interface

D) To improve security

69. How are IPv6 addresses assigned to an interface?

A) Using the command "ipv6 address"

B) Using the command "ip address"

C) Using the command "ipconfig"

Copyright © 2024 VERSAtile Reads. All rights reserved.

This material is protected by copyright, any infringement will be dealt with legal and punitive action.

D) Using the command "ifconfig"

70. What is the administrative distance (AD) of connected routes?

A) Zero

B) One

C) Infinity

D) Ten

71. Which type of route entry provides a simplified static default route?

A) Connected route

B) Static route

C) Dynamic route

D) Default-gateway route

72. How does a device determine the destination MAC address when forwarding packets to a different network?

A) By using ARP

B) By using ICMP

C) By using DNS

D) By using DHCP

73. In the Layer 3 forwarding process, what does the source device identify from its local routing table?

A) Destination IP address

B) Source IP address

C) Next-hop IP address

D) Destination MAC address

Copyright © 2024 VERSAtile Reads. All rights reserved.

This material is protected by copyright, any infringement will be dealt with legal and punitive action. 35

74. Which command is used to clear the MAC address table for the entire switch?

A) clear mac address-table dynamic

B) mac address-table static

C) show interfaces switchport

D) show interface status

75. What is the purpose of the "show interfaces switchport" command?

A) To view the ARP table

B) To view the MAC address table

C) To view the switch port status

D) To view Layer 3 forwarding details

76. What does the "Access Mode VLAN" field indicate?

A) The VLAN assigned to the access port

B) The VLAN assigned to the trunk port

C) The VLAN assigned to the management port

D) The VLAN assigned to the voice port

77. What does the "Status" field in the "show interface status" command indicate?

A) Port duplex

B) Port speed

C) Port VLAN

D) Port connectivity

Copyright © 2024 VERSAtile Reads. All rights reserved.

This material is protected by copyright, any infringement will be dealt with legal and punitive action.

78. What does the Address Resolution Protocol (ARP) table map?

A) Layer 2 MAC addresses to Layer 1 physical addresses

B) Layer 3 IP addresses to Layer 4 port numbers

C) Layer 3 IP addresses to Layer 2 MAC addresses

D) Layer 2 MAC addresses to Layer 3 IP addresses

79. What is one key advantage of site-to-site IPsec VPNs?

A) Easy to manage in large networks

B) Supports multivendor interoperability

C) Provides unencrypted traffic

D) Uses proprietary encryption standards

80. Which technology simplifies configuration for hub-and-spoke and spoke-to-spoke VPNs?

A) Site-to-site IPsec VPNs

B) Cisco Group Encrypted Transport VPN (GET VPN)

C) Cisco Dynamic Multipoint VPN (DMVPN)

D) Remote VPN Access

81. What combination does Cisco DMVPN use to simplify VPN configuration?

A) IPsec and L2TP

B) GRE and PPTP

C) mGRE, IPsec, and NHRP

D) SSL and TLS

82. Cisco GET VPN is designed for which type of networks?

Copyright © 2024 VERSAtile Reads. All rights reserved.

This material is protected by copyright, any infringement will be dealt with legal and punitive action.

A) Public internet

B) Service provider MPLS networks

C) Wireless networks

D) Personal home networks

83. What is a unique feature of Cisco GET VPN?

A) Creates any-to-any tunnel-less VPNs

B) Requires new MPLS network services

C) Only supports unicast traffic

D) Does not comply with regulatory guidelines

84. What regulatory compliance guidelines does Cisco GET VPN help address?

A) GDPR

B) HIPAA, Sarbanes-Oxley, PCI DSS, GLBA

C) CCPA

D) FISMA

85. What is Cisco FlexVPN's main feature?

A) Uses IKEv1 standard

B) Only supports remote access VPNs

C) Combines multiple VPN topologies

D) Requires hardware-based encryption

86. Which VPN solution allows remote users to securely access a corporate network?

A) Cisco GET VPN

Copyright © 2024 VERSAtile Reads. All rights reserved.
This material is protected by copyright, any infringement will be dealt with legal and punitive action.

B) Cisco DMVPN

C) Site-to-site IPsec VPN

D) Remote VPN Access

87. Why is GRE over IPsec used?

A) For data compression

B) To provide encryption and authentication for GRE tunnels

C) To increase network speed

D) For network address translation

88. What is a major limitation of using crypto maps for IPsec tunnel protection?

A) Supports MPLS natively

B) Configuration is simple

C) Consumes excessive TCAM space

D) Is no longer widely deployed

89. In IPsec configuration, which command is used to classify VPN traffic?

A) ip access-list extended

B) crypto isakmp policy

C) crypto ipsec transform-set

D) tunnel protection ipsec profile

90. Which encryption algorithms are no longer recommended for ISAKMP policy?

A) AES and 3DES

B) DES and MD5

Copyright © 2024 VERSAtile Reads. All rights reserved.

This material is protected by copyright, any infringement will be dealt with legal and punitive action.

C) SHA and AES 256

D) RSA and DH group 24

91. What is the purpose of the 'crypto isakmp key' command?

A) To define the transform set

B) To configure the pre-shared key (PSK)

C) To set the encryption algorithm

D) To create an access list

92. Which ISAKMP encryption algorithm is recommended over DES and 3DES?

A) MD5

B) SHA

C) AES

D) RSA

93. What is an IPsec profile used for?

A) To define the global pool of IP addresses for NAT

B) To apply a crypto map to an interface

C) To specify transform sets for IPsec negotiation

D) To configure GRE tunnels

94. How is an IPsec profile applied to a tunnel interface?

A) Using the 'crypto map' command

B) Using the 'tunnel protection ipsec profile' command

C) Using the 'ip access-list extended' command

Copyright © 2024 VERSAtile Reads. All rights reserved.

This material is protected by copyright, any infringement will be dealt with legal and punitive action. 40

D) Using the 'crypto isakmp key' command

95. Which protocol does LISP improve in terms of load sharing by preventing polarization?

A) TCP

B) UDP

C) ICMP

D) GRE

96. What is one of the main reasons traditional Layer 2 networks face issues with server virtualization?

A) Limited VLAN ID space

B) Limited IP address space

C) Inadequate UDP port numbers

D) Limited number of MAC addresses

97. Which of the following statements is true regarding the VXLAN UDP destination port?

A) The default UDP destination port used by Linux is 4789.

B) IANA assigned port 8472 for VXLAN.

C) The default UDP destination port used by Linux is 8472.

D) VXLAN does not use UDP.

98. How many VXLAN segments can coexist within the same infrastructure?

A) 4000

B) 16,000

Copyright © 2024 VERSAtile Reads. All rights reserved.

This material is protected by copyright, any infringement will be dealt with legal and punitive action.

C) 1 million

D) 16 million

99. What is the primary purpose of the Spanning Tree Protocol (STP)?

A) To increase network speed

B) To prevent loops in Layer 2 networks

C) To prioritize network traffic

D) To improve network security

100. Which of the following is NOT a port state in the 802.1D STP protocol?

A) Disabled

B) Listening

C) Forwarding

D) Disconnected

101. In STP, what is the purpose of the Root Port (RP)?

A) To forward traffic toward the root bridge

B) To block traffic on redundant ports

C) To receive and forward BPDUs

D) To determine the root bridge

102. What does a Blocking port state indicate in STP?

A) The port is forwarding traffic.

B) The port is shut down administratively.

C) The port is listening for BPDUs.

D) The port is not forwarding traffic to prevent loops.

Copyright © 2024 VERSAtile Reads. All rights reserved.
This material is protected by copyright, any infringement will be dealt with legal and punitive action.

103. How long does it typically take for a port to enter the Forwarding state in 802.1D STP using default timers?

A) 5 seconds

B) 15 seconds

C) 20 seconds

D) 30 seconds

104. Which of the following is NOT a key term related to STP?

A) Root bridge

B) Routing table

C) BPDU

D) Root path cost

105. What does the Max Age timer determine in STP?

A) The maximum age of a BPDU packet

B) The time before a port transitions to the Forwarding state

C) The time a switch waits to hear from the root bridge

D) The time before a switch discards BPDU information

106. Which STP port type connects to the root bridge or an upstream switch in the spanning-tree topology?

A) Root port (RP)

B) Designated port (DP)

C) Blocking port

D) Listening port

Copyright © 2024 VERSAtile Reads. All rights reserved.

This material is protected by copyright, any infringement will be dealt with legal and punitive action. 43

107. What is the purpose of the Bridge Protocol Data Unit (BPDU)?

A) To forward network traffic

B) To identify a hierarchy and notify of topology changes

C) To establish a secure connection between switches

D) To configure VLANs in a network

108. What is the main function of Rapid Spanning Tree Protocol (RSTP)?

A) To improve convergence time in the spanning tree topology

B) To prioritize certain types of network traffic

C) To increase the number of VLANs supported by STP

D) To encrypt BPDU packets for secure communication

109. What is the primary purpose of Spanning Tree Protocol (STP) in a network environment?

A) To increase network bandwidth

B) To prevent Layer 2 loops

C) To prioritize network traffic

D) To improve network security

110. Which IEEE standard originally defined the Spanning Tree Protocol?

A) 802.11

B) 802.1D

C) 802.3ae

D) 802.1X

111. What is the function of a Root Port (RP) in STP?

Copyright © 2024 VERSAtile Reads. All rights reserved.
This material is protected by copyright, any infringement will be dealt with legal and punitive action.

A) Receives and forwards BPDU frames

B) Connects to the root bridge or an upstream switch

C) Temporarily blocks traffic on redundant ports

D) Initiates the STP tree-based algorithm

112. Which STP port state allows the switch port to forward network traffic?

A) Blocking

B) Listening

C) Learning

D) Forwarding

113. What does the Max Age parameter in STP determine?

A) The maximum length of time for a port to enter the forwarding state

B) The time that a BPDU is advertised out of a port

C) The time before a bridge port saves its BPDU information

D) The maximum number of MAC addresses allowed in the address table

114. Which STP port type connects to downstream devices and switches?

A) Root port (RP)

B) Designated port (DP)

C) Blocking port

D) Trunk port

115. What is the significance of the System ID Extension in STP?

A) It indicates the preference for a switch to be the root bridge

B) It identifies the VLAN that the BPDU correlates to

Copyright © 2024 VERSAtile Reads. All rights reserved.
This material is protected by copyright, any infringement will be dealt with legal and punitive action.

VERSAtile Reads

C) It specifies the maximum length of time before a bridge port saves its BPDU information

D) It determines the forwarding delay for a port

116. Which STP mode is backward compatible with IEEE 802.1D?

A) PVST+

B) RSTP

C) MST

D) PVST

117. How does STP determine the Root Bridge in a network?

A) By selecting the switch with the lowest MAC address

B) By selecting the switch with the highest priority

C) By running a tree-based algorithm

D) By analyzing the topology changes

118. Which STP port type forwards traffic toward the root bridge or an upstream switch?

A) Root port (RP)

B) Designated port (DP)

C) Blocking port

D) Trunk port

119. What is the main purpose of the Configuration BPDU in STP?

A) To identify the root bridge and root ports

B) To communicate changes in the Layer 2 topology

C) To specify the maximum age of a BPDU

Copyright © 2024 VERSAtile Reads. All rights reserved.
This material is protected by copyright, any infringement will be dealt with legal and punitive action.

D) To determine the maximum length of time before a bridge port saves its BPDU information

120. Which STP port state allows the switch port to receive BPDUs and send its own BPDUs?

A) Listening

B) Blocking

C) Learning

D) Forwarding

121. What parameter does STP use to calculate the combined cost for a specific path toward the root switch?

A) Root bridge identifier

B) Max Age

C) System priority

D) Root path cost

122. Which STP port state indicates a major configuration or operational problem on a port?

A) Broken

B) Forwarding

C) Learning

D) Blocking

123. How does STP handle redundant ports to ensure a loop-free topology?

A) By blocking traffic on all ports except the root port

B) By disabling all redundant ports permanently

Copyright © 2024 VERSAtile Reads. All rights reserved.
This material is protected by copyright, any infringement will be dealt with legal and punitive action.

C) By dynamically selecting specific ports to block temporarily

D) By forwarding traffic on all ports simultaneously

124. What happens during the Learning state of an STP port?

A) The port can forward all network traffic

B) The port modifies the MAC address table with network traffic

C) The port discards packets due to a major problem

D) The port receives BPDUs but cannot forward any other network traffic

125. What determines the preference for a switch to become the root bridge in STP?

A) The number of ports on the switch

B) The highest system priority value

C) The lowest system MAC address

D) The number of VLANs configured on the switch

126. What is the primary purpose of the Topology Change Notification (TCN) BPDU in STP?

A) To identify the root bridge

B) To communicate changes in the Layer 2 topology

C) To specify the maximum age of a BPDU

D) To determine the maximum length of time before a bridge port saves its BPDU information

127. Which STP port state is considered the final state for a switch port to forward network traffic?

A) Listening

Copyright © 2024 VERSAtile Reads. All rights reserved.
This material is protected by copyright, any infringement will be dealt with legal and punitive action.

B) Blocking

C) Learning

D) Forwarding

128. What determines the duration of the Learning state in STP?

A) Hello time

B) Max Age

C) Forward delay

D) Root path cost

129. Which STP mode is primarily used for ensuring a loop-free topology for one VLAN?

A) PVST

B) RSTP

C) MST

D) 802.1D

130. How does STP prevent loops in a network topology?

A) By permanently disabling redundant ports

B) By dynamically blocking specific ports temporarily

C) By forwarding traffic on all ports simultaneously

D) By continuously monitoring network bandwidth usage

131. What does the System Priority parameter in STP indicate?

A) The preference for a switch to be the root bridge

B) The maximum length of time before a bridge port saves its BPDU information

Copyright © 2024 VERSAtile Reads. All rights reserved.
This material is protected by copyright, any infringement will be dealt with legal and punitive action.

C) The number of VLANs configured on the switch

D) The priority for forwarding network traffic

132. What determines the duration of the Blocking state in STP?

A) Forward delay

B) Max Age

C) Hello time

D) System Priority

133. Which STP port type receives and forwards BPDU frames to other switches?

A) Root port (RP)

B) Designated port (DP)

C) Blocking port

D) Trunk port

134. What is an Autonomous System (AS)?

A) A collection of routers under a single organization's control

B) A network protocol used for internet routing

C) A type of IP address

D) A hardware component in routers

135. Which protocol is used for internal routing within an AS?

A) BGP

B) IGP

C) EGP

Copyright © 2024 VERSAtile Reads. All rights reserved.

This material is protected by copyright, any infringement will be dealt with legal and punitive action. 50

D) MPLS

136. What is the purpose of the Autonomous System Number (ASN)?

A) To uniquely identify a network interface

B) To uniquely identify an AS

C) To provide IP addresses to devices

D) To establish a routing protocol

137. How many ASNs are available in the original 16-bit ASN range?

A) 32,768

B) 65,535

C) 128,000

D) 4,294,967,295

138. Which organization is responsible for assigning public ASNs?

A) IETF

B) ICANN

C) IANA

D) ISO

139. What type of Path Attribute (PA) is mandatory in BGP?

A) Well-known discretionary

B) Optional transitive

C) Well-known mandatory

D) Optional non-transitive

Copyright © 2024 VERSAtile Reads. All rights reserved.
This material is protected by copyright, any infringement will be dealt with legal and punitive action. 51

140. What does the AS_Path attribute in BGP prevent?

A) IP address duplication

B) Routing loops

C) Unauthorized access

D) Packet loss

141. What are the two identifiers used in Multi-Protocol BGP (MP-BGP)?

A) AFI and SAFI

B) API and SPI

C) IP and MAC

D) TCP and UDP

142. On which TCP port does BGP communication occur?

A) 80

B) 443

C) 179

D) 8080

143. Which type of BGP session is used within the same AS?

A) eBGP

B) iBGP

C) mBGP

D) sBGP

144. What is the Administrative Distance (AD) of eBGP?

A) 90

Copyright © 2024 VERSAtile Reads. All rights reserved.

This material is protected by copyright, any infringement will be dealt with legal and punitive action. 52

B) 100

C) 200

D) 20

145. What state does a BGP session start in?

A) Connect

B) Active

C) Idle

D) Established

146. What is the default TTL value for eBGP sessions?

A) 64

B) 1

C) 32

D) 128

147. Which command initializes BGP in the router configuration?

A) router ospf

B) router bgp

C) bgp router-id

D) network bgp

148. What command identifies a BGP neighbor?

A) neighbor ip-address remote-as as-number

B) router-id

C) network prefix mask

Copyright © 2024 VERSAtile Reads. All rights reserved.
This material is protected by copyright, any infringement will be dealt with legal and punitive action. 53

D) neighbor activate

149. Which Address Family Identifier (AFI) is used for IPv6?

A) 1

B) 2

C) 3

D) 4

150. What is the default Administrative Distance (AD) of iBGP?

A) 90

B) 110

C) 200

D) 20

151. What does MP_REACH_NLRI stand for?

A) Multi-Protocol Reachable Network Layer Reachability Information

B) Multi-Protocol Reachable Next Layer Reachability Information

C) Multi-Protocol Reachable Network Layer Routing Information

D) Multi-Protocol Reachable Network Logical Routing Information

152. What happens if a BGP router detects its own ASN in the AS_Path attribute?

A) It forwards the prefix

B) It discards the prefix

C) It modifies the prefix

D) It sends an error message

Copyright © 2024 VERSAtile Reads. All rights reserved.
This material is protected by copyright, any infringement will be dealt with legal and punitive action. 54

VERSAtile Reads

153. Which type of Path Attribute is not shared between ASs?

A) Well-known discretionary

B) Optional transitive

C) Well-known mandatory

D) Optional non-transitive

154. What is required for iBGP to function properly in an AS?

A) Full mesh of iBGP peers

B) Single eBGP connection

C) Multiple ASNs

D) Private IP addressing

155. Which statement is true about BGP loop prevention?

A) It uses the Next-Hop attribute

B) It uses the AS_Path attribute

C) It uses the Local_Pref attribute

D) It uses the MED attribute

156. What is a well-known mandatory attribute in BGP?

A) AS_Path

B) Community

C) Local_Pref

D) MED

157. How does BGP differ from IGPs in terms of hop limit?

Copyright © 2024 VERSAtile Reads. All rights reserved.
This material is protected by copyright, any infringement will be dealt with legal and punitive action.

A) BGP has no hop limit by default

B) BGP has a hop limit of 15

C) BGP has a hop limit of 255

D) BGP has a hop limit of 64

158. What command initializes the Address Family in BGP?

A) address-family afi safi

B) router bgp address-family

C) network address-family

D) bgp address-family

159. What does BGP use to manage session states?

A) State Transition Protocol

B) Finite State Machine (FSM)

C) Session Management Protocol

D) Network State Manager

160. What is the significance of the TTL value in eBGP sessions?

A) It limits the distance of the BGP session

B) It enhances security

C) It ensures session reliability

D) It improves performance

161. Which address family does AFI=1 represent?

A) IPv4

B) IPv6

Copyright © 2024 VERSAtile Reads. All rights reserved.

This material is protected by copyright, any infringement will be dealt with legal and punitive action.

C) MPLS

D) VPNv4

162. What is the command to define a router ID in BGP?

A) bgp router-id

B) router bgp

C) network router-id

D) router-id bgp

163. How are prefixes advertised in BGP?

A) Using OSPF network statements

B) Using BGP network statements

C) Using RIP network statements

D) Using static routes

164. What is the Administrative Distance (AD) of OSPF?

A) 90

B) 110

C) 120

D) 200

165. Which path attribute influences BGP route selection by preferring shorter AS paths?

A) Local_Pref

B) MED

C) AS_Path

Copyright © 2024 VERSAtile Reads. All rights reserved.

This material is protected by copyright, any infringement will be dealt with legal and punitive action.

D) Community

166. What type of path attribute is "Local_Pref" in BGP?

A) Well-known mandatory

B) Well-known discretionary

C) Optional transitive

D) Optional non-transitive

167. Which BGP session type typically requires manual peering configuration?

A) iBGP

B) eBGP

C) MP-BGP

D) VPN-BGP

168. What does the 'Established' state in a BGP session indicate?

A) The session is attempting to connect

B) The session is active but not fully formed

C) The session is fully operational

D) The session has failed

169. What is a valid private 16-bit ASN range?

A) 1–64,511

B) 65,536–131,071

C) 64,512–65,535

D) 131,072–262,143

Copyright © 2024 VERSAtile Reads. All rights reserved.
This material is protected by copyright, any infringement will be dealt with legal and punitive action.

170. How is the "Community" attribute classified in BGP?

A) Well-known mandatory

B) Well-known discretionary

C) Optional transitive

D) Optional non-transitive

171. What does the 'OpenSent' state signify in a BGP session?

A) A BGP message is being sent

B) A BGP message is being received

C) The session is closed

D) The session is established

172. Which command activates an address family for a BGP neighbor?

A) neighbor ip-address activate

B) neighbor activate

C) router bgp activate

D) address-family activate

173. What function does the Next-Hop attribute serve in BGP?

A) It specifies the next router in the path

B) It prevents routing loops

C) It determines route preference

D) It provides metric information

Copyright © 2024 VERSAtile Reads. All rights reserved.
This material is protected by copyright, any infringement will be dealt with legal and punitive action.

174. Which BGP attribute can be used to control route advertisement within an AS?

A) AS_Path

B) Local_Pref

C) MED

D) Community

175. What is the purpose of the network command in BGP configuration?

A) To define BGP neighbors

B) To specify the router ID

C) To advertise network prefixes

D) To configure AS numbers

176. Which BGP state indicates that the session has failed?

A) Idle

B) Connect

C) Active

D) Established

177. What is the role of the Finite State Machine (FSM) in BGP?

A) To route data packets

B) To manage routing tables

C) To control BGP session states

D) To establish TCP connections

178. Which attribute is used by BGP to determine the best path when multiple routes are available?

Copyright © 2024 VERSAtile Reads. All rights reserved.

This material is protected by copyright, any infringement will be dealt with legal and punitive action.

A) MED

B) Next-Hop

C) AS_Path

D) Local_Pref

179. What is the command to specify the remote AS for a BGP neighbor?

A) neighbor remote-as

B) router remote-as

C) remote-as neighbor

D) bgp remote-as

180. Which attribute is used to prevent BGP loops by listing the ASs traversed?

A) Next-Hop

B) AS_Path

C) Local_Pref

D) Community

181. What is the default TTL value for iBGP sessions?

A) 1

B) 64

C) 128

D) 255

182. What does the command bgp router-id router-id do?

A) Sets the router ID for BGP

Copyright © 2024 VERSAtile Reads. All rights reserved.

This material is protected by copyright, any infringement will be dealt with legal and punitive action.

B) Specifies the BGP neighbor

C) Activates an address family

D) Defines the network prefix

183. Which BGP session type has a default Administrative Distance (AD) of 20?

A) iBGP

B) eBGP

C) MP-BGP

D) VPN-BGP

184. What is BGP multi-homing?

A) Using multiple service providers for redundancy

B) Establishing multiple BGP sessions across different peering links

C) Advertising all routes to the RIB

D) Filtering routes using ACLs

185. What is the default behavior of BGP regarding route advertisement?

A) Advertise all possible paths

B) Advertise only the best path

C) Advertise paths based on cost

D) Advertise paths based on availability

186. Which BGP attribute defines the IP address to which BGP packets should be forwarded next in order to reach a destination network?

Copyright © 2024 VERSAtile Reads. All rights reserved.

This material is protected by copyright, any infringement will be dealt with legal and punitive action.

A) Local Preference
B) AS Path
C) Next Hop
D) Weight

187. Why might an organization choose to use different service providers for each circuit?

A) To reduce the number of BGP sessions

B) To optimize routing traffic using the BGP best-path algorithm

C) To minimize cost and maximize circuit availability

D) To simplify network management

188. Which type of IPv6 address is used for one-to-many communication within a specified group of devices?

A) Unicast

B) Multicast

C) Anycast

D) Broadcast

189. Which protocol is commonly used to automate the deployment, configuration, and management of network devices in a Cisco network?

A) OSPF

B) BGP

C) SNMP

D) Cisco DNA Center

190. How can transit routing be avoided in a multi-homed environment?

A) By using a single service provider

Copyright © 2024 VERSAtile Reads. All rights reserved.
This material is protected by copyright, any infringement will be dealt with legal and punitive action.

B) By configuring outbound route filtering at each branch site

C) By establishing iBGP sessions

D) By not advertising any routes to the WAN

191. What problem might occur if transit routers' circuits become oversaturated?

A) Suboptimal routing

B) Increased link failures

C) Unpredictable and nondeterministic routing patterns

D) Reduced redundancy

192. What is the main purpose of Access Control Lists (ACLs) in routing protocols?

A) To filter packets based on quality of service

B) To classify packets for routing protocol identification

C) To provide basic firewall functionality

D) To optimize routing traffic

193. What is the default action for packets that do not match any ACE in an ACL?

A) Permit

B) Deny

C) Reroute

D) Log

194. Which of the following is a feature of standard ACLs?

A) They define packets based on source and destination

Copyright © 2024 VERSAtile Reads. All rights reserved.

This material is protected by copyright, any infringement will be dealt with legal and punitive action.

B) They use numbered entries 1–99 or 1300–1999

C) They use numbered entries 100–199 or 2000–2699

D) They filter based on protocol and port

195. What does the 'any' keyword in an ACL replace?

A) A specific IP address

B) 0.0.0.0 0.0.0.0

C) A subnet mask

D) A host address

196. How are prefix lists different from ACLs in routing protocols?

A) Prefix lists use high-order bit patterns for matching

B) Prefix lists filter packets based on source and destination

C) ACLs are preferred over prefix lists for network selection

D) Prefix lists only define exact matches

197. What component of a route map dictates the processing order?

A) Conditional matching criteria

B) Processing action

C) Sequence number

D) Optional action

198. What is the default processing action in a route map if not specified?

A) Deny

B) Permit

C) Log

Copyright © 2024 VERSAtile Reads. All rights reserved.
This material is protected by copyright, any infringement will be dealt with legal and punitive action.

D) Reroute

199. What is a potential consequence of improper transit routing design?

A) Oversaturated circuits

B) Improved traffic flow

C) Simplified troubleshooting

D) Reduced redundancy

200. Which QoS technique is used to ensure a minimum level of service to critical applications by reserving bandwidth?

A) Traffic Shaping

B) Traffic Policing

C) Resource Reservation Protocol (RSVP)

D) Weighted Fair Queuing (WFQ)

201. What is the purpose of setting a higher local preference for MPLS SP2 in branch transit routing?

A) To filter traffic

B) To prefer routing through MPLS SP2

C) To block routing through MPLS SP1

D) To establish redundancy

202. Which component of a route map allows for modification, addition, or removal of route characteristics?

A) Sequence number

B) Conditional matching criteria

C) Processing action

Copyright © 2024 VERSAtile Reads. All rights reserved.

This material is protected by copyright, any infringement will be dealt with legal and punitive action.

D) Optional action

203. How can routing patterns become unpredictable in a multi-homed design?

A) By configuring multiple eBGP sessions

B) By allowing routers to act as transit routers

C) By optimizing traffic using the best-path algorithm

D) By setting different local preferences

204. What does a high-order bit pattern in a prefix list represent?

A) The network address

B) The subnet mask

C) The length or mask length

D) The IP address

205. Why are named ACLs generally preferred?

A) They are easier to manage and remember

B) They provide more filtering options

C) They use a simpler syntax

D) They are more secure

206. What is the main reason for using route maps in BGP?

A) To filter out unwanted routes

B) To modify routing policies on a per-neighbor basis

C) To simplify BGP configuration

D) To ensure network security

Copyright © 2024 VERSAtile Reads. All rights reserved.
This material is protected by copyright, any infringement will be dealt with legal and punitive action.

207. Which of the following is NOT a characteristic of a sequence number in a route map?

A) It is mandatory to specify

B) It dictates the processing order

C) It increments by 10 automatically if not specified

D) It can be omitted in the configuration

208. What type of ACL defines packets based solely on the source network?

A) Standard ACL

B) Extended ACL

C) Named ACL

D) Prefix list

209. What action is taken when a match is found in an ACL?

A) Continue processing the next ACE

B) Stop processing and take the appropriate action

C) Log the packet details

D) Forward the packet to a default route

210. What happens if a sequence number is not provided in a route map statement?

A) The sequence number is set to 0

B) The statement is ignored

C) The sequence number increments by 10 automatically

D) An error is generated

Copyright © 2024 VERSAtile Reads. All rights reserved.
This material is protected by copyright, any infringement will be dealt with legal and punitive action. 68

211. How does using multiple service providers affect routing in BGP?

A) It simplifies routing

B) It enhances redundancy and optimization

C) It reduces the number of BGP sessions

D) It complicates routing decisions

212. Why is transit routing undesirable in branch sites?

A) It increases network complexity

B) It can lead to oversaturated circuits

C) It simplifies troubleshooting

D) It enhances traffic optimization

213. What is the implicit rule at the end of every ACL?

A) Permit all traffic

B) Deny all traffic

C) Log all traffic

D) Forward all traffic to a default route

214. How can you prevent a branch router from acting as a transit router?

A) By using multiple eBGP sessions

B) By configuring outbound route filtering

C) By setting a higher local preference

D) By using only one service provider

215. What is the role of a prefix match specification in a prefix list?

A) To filter packets based on source and destination

Copyright © 2024 VERSAtile Reads. All rights reserved.
This material is protected by copyright, any infringement will be dealt with legal and punitive action.

B) To define the bit pattern and length for matching

C) To classify packets for quality of service

D) To optimize routing traffic

216. In an ACL, what does the host keyword refer to?

A) A specific protocol

B) A /32 IP address

C) A source network

D) A subnet mask

217. What happens to traffic if the transit router's circuits become oversaturated?

A) Traffic is rerouted automatically

B) Routing patterns become unpredictable

C) Redundancy is increased

D) Traffic is filtered

218. Which protocol is used by EIGRP to send hello packets and updates?

A) TCP

B) UDP

C) IP

D) RTP

219. What is a common use of ACLs besides filtering packets?

A) Providing basic firewall functionality

B) Identifying networks within routing protocols

Copyright © 2024 VERSAtile Reads. All rights reserved.
This material is protected by copyright, any infringement will be dealt with legal and punitive action.

C) Optimizing routing traffic

D). Establishing BGP sessions

220. How can routing patterns be made predictable in a multi-homed environment?

A) By avoiding transit routing

B) By using multiple service providers

C) By setting the same local preference for all routes

D) By configuring static routes

221. What is the main function of the conditional matching criteria in a route map?

A) To dictate the processing order

B) To permit or deny the prefix

C) To identify prefix characteristics

D) To add or modify route characteristics

222. Why might an organization prefer using prefix lists over ACLs in routing protocols?

A) Prefix lists are simpler to configure

B) Prefix lists provide more detailed network selection

C) ACLs cannot filter based on source and destination

D) ACLs are less secure

223. What is the purpose of the processing action in a route map?

A) To dictate the order of route map statements

B) To permit or deny the prefix

Copyright © 2024 VERSAtile Reads. All rights reserved.

This material is protected by copyright, any infringement will be dealt with legal and punitive action. 71

C) To identify matching criteria

D) To modify route attributes

224. Which technology is used to combine multiple Ethernet links into a single logical link, providing increased bandwidth and redundancy?

A) LACP
B) VTP
C) STP
D) OSPF

225. How can a network design accommodate outages effectively?

A) By using a single service provider

B) By sizing bandwidth accordingly

C) By configuring static routes

D) By avoiding transit routing

226. What is the role of AS path ACLs in conditional matching?

A) To filter packets based on the source network

B) To classify packets for quality of service

C) To identify networks within routing protocols

D) To match routes based on AS path attributes

227. How does the sequence number in a route map affect processing?

A) It identifies prefix characteristics

B) It determines the processing order

C) It permits or denies the prefix

Copyright © 2024 VERSAtile Reads. All rights reserved.
This material is protected by copyright, any infringement will be dealt with legal and punitive action.

D) It adds or modifies route characteristics

228. Why is setting a higher local preference for MPLS SP2 important in branch transit routing?

A) To avoid transit routing

B) To prefer routing through MPLS SP2

C) To filter out unwanted routes

D) To establish redundancy

229. What is the potential benefit of using different service providers for each circuit?

A) Simplified network management

B) Increased cost savings

C) Enhanced redundancy and optimization

D) Reduced number of BGP sessions

230. What is the purpose of the OSPF "router-id" command?

A) To identify the OSPF process ID

B) To uniquely identify the router in the OSPF domain

C) To set the priority of the router in the OSPF election

D) To configure the router's IP address

231. What is the purpose of the OSPF "router-id" command?

A) To identify the OSPF process ID

B) To uniquely identify the router in the OSPF domain

C) To set the priority of the router in the OSPF election

D) To configure the router's IP address

Copyright © 2024 VERSAtile Reads. All rights reserved.
This material is protected by copyright, any infringement will be dealt with legal and punitive action.

232. Which OSPF area type allows for the redistribution of external routes but does not propagate Type 5 LSAs?

A) Backbone Area

B) Stub Area

C) Not-So-Stubby Area (NSSA)

D) Totally Stubby Area

233. Which command is used to initiate a hard reset of a BGP session?

A) clear ip bgp ip-address

B) clear ip bgp ip-address soft

C) clear bgp afi safi ip-address

D) clear bgp session ip-address

234. What does a soft reset in BGP do?

A) Tears down the BGP session

B) Removes BGP routes from the peer

C) Invalidates the BGP cache and requests a full advertisement

D) Shuts down the router

235. How can all of a router's BGP sessions be cleared simultaneously?

A) clear bgp all

B) clear ip bgp *

C) clear bgp afi safi all

D) clear all bgp

Copyright © 2024 VERSAtile Reads. All rights reserved.
This material is protected by copyright, any infringement will be dealt with legal and punitive action.

236. What capability allows a BGP peer to re-advertise prefixes to a requesting router?

A) Hard reset

B) Soft reset

C) Route refresh

D) Local preference

237. Which command initiates a soft reset for a specific address family in BGP?

A) clear ip bgp ip-address

B) clear bgp afi safi ip-address

C) clear bgp afi safi ip-address soft [in | out]

D) clear bgp session ip-address soft [in | out]

238. What is the purpose of BGP communities?

A) To tear down BGP sessions

B) To tag routes and modify BGP routing policy

C) To request a full advertisement from a BGP peer

D) To refresh BGP routes

239. What is the format of a private BGP community?

A) (0-4,294,967,295)

B) (0-65535):(0-65535)

C) (0-65535):(0-4,294,967,295)

D) (4,294,901,760-4,294,967,295)

Copyright © 2024 VERSAtile Reads. All rights reserved.
This material is protected by copyright, any infringement will be dealt with legal and punitive action.

240. Which RFC expanded BGP communities' capabilities to include an extended format?

A) RFC 1112

B) RFC 2236

C) RFC 3376

D) RFC 4360

241. Which well-known BGP community indicates routes that should not be advertised to any BGP peer?

A) Internet

B) No_Advertise

C) No_Export

D) All_Advertise

242. How are standard BGP communities enabled on a neighbor-by-neighbor basis?

A) By default

B) Using the command neighbor ip-address send-community

C) Using the command neighbor ip-address receive-community

D) Using the command neighbor ip-address enable-community

243. What is the first step in the BGP best-path selection algorithm?

A) Local preference

B) Weight

C) AS_Path

D) MED

Copyright © 2024 VERSAtile Reads. All rights reserved.

This material is protected by copyright, any infringement will be dealt with legal and punitive action.

244. Which attribute in the BGP best-path algorithm is Cisco-defined and not advertised to other routers?

A) Local preference

B) Weight

C) AS_Path

D) MED

245. What attribute indicates the preference for exiting the AS to the destination network?

A) Weight

B) Local preference

C) AS_Path

D) MED

246. Which BGP attribute is non-transitive and influences traffic flows inbound from a different AS?

A) Weight

B) Local preference

C) AS_Path

D) MED

247. Which command displays the BGP table for a specific network prefix on a router?

A) show ip bgp

B) show bgp afi safi

C) show ip route bgp

D) show bgp summary

Copyright © 2024 VERSAtile Reads. All rights reserved.

This material is protected by copyright, any infringement will be dealt with legal and punitive action. 77

248. What is the purpose of the AIGP metric in BGP?

A) To identify the preference for outbound traffic

B) To provide a path metric in environments with multiple ASs

C) To prepend ASNs to the AS path

D) To set the MED value automatically

249. Which protocol is used to dynamically discover and manage network devices in a Cisco network?

A) LLDP
B) CDP
C) SNMP
D) DHCP

250. What is the default local preference value if not defined by the edge BGP router?

A) 0

B) 50

C) 100

D) 200

251. Which attribute is used to identify the shortest path to a destination in BGP?

A) Weight

B) Local preference

C) AS_Path

D) MED

Copyright © 2024 VERSAtile Reads. All rights reserved.
This material is protected by copyright, any infringement will be dealt with legal and punitive action.

252. How can an organization influence the path selection for outbound traffic using BGP?

A) By setting the weight attribute

B) By modifying the AS_Path attribute

C) By setting the local preference attribute

D) By changing the MED value

253. Which BGP community value signifies that routes should not be advertised to any eBGP peer?

A) Internet

B) No_Advertise

C) No_Export

D) Local_Preference

254. What does the prefix length determine in BGP routing path selection?

A) The shortest AS path

B) The highest local preference

C) The longest match

D) The lowest MED

255. How are BGP routes with a longer matching prefix handled in path selection?

A) They are preferred over shorter prefixes

B) They are preferred over shorter AS paths

C) They are ignored in preference to shorter prefixes

D) They are preferred over higher MED values

Copyright © 2024 VERSAtile Reads. All rights reserved.

This material is protected by copyright, any infringement will be dealt with legal and punitive action.

256. What does the command clear bgp afi safi {ip-address|*} soft [in | out] do?

A) Initiates a hard reset of BGP sessions

B) Initiates a soft reset for a specific address family

C) Clears all BGP routes from the routing table

D) Displays the BGP table for a specific network prefix

257. Which BGP attribute is evaluated first in the best-path selection algorithm?

A) Weight

B) Local preference

C) AS_Path

D) MED

258. What is the default behavior for advertising BGP communities in IOS and IOS XE routers?

A) They are advertised to all peers

B) They are not advertised by default

C) They are advertised to iBGP peers only

D) They are advertised to eBGP peers only

259. How is a BGP community displayed in the new format?

A) As a 32-bit number

B) As two 16-bit numbers separated by a colon

C) As a hexadecimal number

D) As an IP address

Copyright © 2024 VERSAtile Reads. All rights reserved.
This material is protected by copyright, any infringement will be dealt with legal and punitive action.

VERSAtile Reads

260. Which BGP attribute is used to influence the path selection process by modifying the preference of routes learned from different ASes?

A) MED

B) Local Preference

C) Weight

D) AS Path

261. Which attribute is commonly used for VPN services in BGP?

A) Standard communities

B) Extended communities

C) Local preference

D) MED

262. How can an organization guarantee deterministic path selection outside the organization?

A) By advertising the same prefix length from all routers

B) By using the shortest AS path

C) By using the highest local preference

D) By advertising a summary prefix and a longer matching prefix

263. What is the purpose of the route refresh capability in BGP?

A) To tear down the BGP session

B) To re-advertise prefixes to the requesting router

C) To reset the local preference

D) To clear all BGP routes

Copyright © 2024 VERSAtile Reads. All rights reserved.
This material is protected by copyright, any infringement will be dealt with legal and punitive action.

VERSAtile Reads

264. Which well-known BGP community value indicates that routes should be advertised on the Internet?

A) Internet

B) No_Advertise

C) No_Export

D) Public

265. How does BGP handle multiple paths to the same destination network?

A) It installs all paths in the RIB

B) It advertises only the best path to neighbors

C) It uses all paths for load balancing

D) It ignores all but the first received path

266. What attribute is compared when there is a tie in the BGP best-path algorithm?

A) Weight

B) Local preference

C) AS_Path

D) Router ID (RID)

267. Which BGP attribute is used to calculate the best path when all other attributes are equal?

A) Weight

B) Local preference

C) Router ID (RID)

D) MED

Copyright © 2024 VERSAtile Reads. All rights reserved.
This material is protected by copyright, any infringement will be dealt with legal and punitive action. 82

268. What is the purpose of the well-known BGP community No_Export?

A) To prevent routes from being advertised to any BGP peer

B) To prevent routes from being advertised to any eBGP peer

C) To prevent routes from being advertised to any iBGP peer

D) To allow routes to be advertised to all peers

269. Which BGP attribute is preferred when the path has the lowest IGP next hop?

A) Weight

B) Local preference

C) AS_Path

D) MED

270. How are routes with higher local preference values treated in the BGP best-path selection?

A) They are less preferred

B) They are preferred

C) They are ignored

D) They are treated the same as lower values

271. What is the effect of the No_Advertise community on BGP routes?

A) Routes are not advertised to any eBGP peer

B) Routes are not advertised to any iBGP peer

C) Routes are not advertised to any BGP peer

D) Routes are advertised to all peers

Copyright © 2024 VERSAtile Reads. All rights reserved.

This material is protected by copyright, any infringement will be dealt with legal and punitive action.

272. Which BGP attribute is used to influence the path chosen for outbound traffic?

A) Weight

B) Local preference

C) AS_Path

D) MED

273. What is the purpose of setting the MED attribute in BGP?

A) To influence the path chosen for inbound traffic

B) To set the local preference for outbound traffic

C) To modify the AS_Path length

D) To set the weight attribute

274. Which command clears a specific BGP session without tearing it down?

A) clear bgp session ip-address

B) clear bgp afi safi ip-address soft [in | out]

C) clear ip bgp ip-address

D) clear ip bgp ip-address soft

275. What is the preferred path if BGP paths have the same weight and local preference?

A) The path with the lowest AS_Path

B) The path with the highest MED

C) The path with the lowest MED

D) The path with the highest AS_Path

Copyright © 2024 VERSAtile Reads. All rights reserved.
This material is protected by copyright, any infringement will be dealt with legal and punitive action.

276. Which command is used to display the BGP table for a specific network prefix?

A) show ip bgp

B) show bgp afi safi

C) show ip route bgp

D) show bgp summary

277. How does a BGP router handle routes with the same prefix length?

A) It prefers the route with the highest MED

B) It prefers the route with the lowest MED

C) It prefers the route with the shortest AS_Path

D) It prefers the route with the highest local preference

278. What is the significance of the AS_Path attribute in BGP?

A) It indicates the length of the path to the destination

B) It indicates the preference for outbound traffic

C) It sets the local preference for inbound traffic

D) It sets the MED for outbound traffic

279. What is the impact of setting a higher local preference for a BGP route?

A) The route is less preferred

B) The route is more preferred

C) The route is ignored

D) The route is advertised to all peers

Copyright © 2024 VERSAtile Reads. All rights reserved.
This material is protected by copyright, any infringement will be dealt with legal and punitive action.

280. Which BGP attribute can be used to modify the AS_Path length for a specific route?

A) Weight

B) Local preference

C) AS_Path

D) MED

281. How can an organization influence the path selection for inbound traffic using BGP?

A) By setting the weight attribute

B) By modifying the AS_Path attribute

C) By setting the local preference attribute

D) By changing the MED value

282. Which command displays the BGP table for a specific address family?

A) show ip bgp

B) show bgp afi safi

C) show ip route bgp

D) show bgp summary

283. Which RFC established common network blocks that should never be seen on the Internet?

A) RFC 1918

B) RFC 2119

C) RFC 2616

D) RFC 822

Copyright © 2024 VERSAtile Reads. All rights reserved.
This material is protected by copyright, any infringement will be dealt with legal and punitive action.

284. How many hosts can the 10.0.0.0/8 network accommodate?

A) 65,536

B) 1,048,576

C) 16,777,216

D) 256

285. What is the size of the 172.16.0.0/24 network?

A) 65,536 hosts

B) 1,048,576 hosts

C) 256 hosts

D) 16,777,216 hosts

286. How many hosts can the 192.168.0.0/16 network accommodate?

A) 16,777,216

B) 65,536

C) 1,048,576

D) 256

287. What is the purpose of Network Address Translation (NAT)?

A) To provide security for private networks

B) To translate domain names into IP addresses

C) To enable private IP networks to connect to the public Internet

D) To assign IP addresses to devices dynamically

288. Which device typically performs NAT?

A) Switch

Copyright © 2024 VERSAtile Reads. All rights reserved.
This material is protected by copyright, any infringement will be dealt with legal and punitive action.

B) Router

C) Hub

D) Modem

289. What does an Inside Local address represent in NAT terminology?

A) The actual private IP address assigned to a device on the inside network

B) The public IP address that represents one or more inside local IP addresses

C) The IP address of an outside host as it appears to the inside network

D) The public IP address assigned to a host on the outside network

290. What is an Inside Global address in NAT?

A) The actual private IP address assigned to a device on the inside network

B) The public IP address that represents one or more inside local IP addresses

C) The IP address of an outside host as it appears to the inside network

D) The public IP address assigned to a host on the outside network

291. What does an Outside Local address represent?

A) The actual private IP address assigned to a device on the inside network

B) The public IP address that represents one or more inside local IP addresses

C) The IP address of an outside host as it appears to the inside network

D) The public IP address assigned to a host on the outside network

292. What is an Outside Global address in NAT terminology?

A) The actual private IP address assigned to a device on the inside network

Copyright © 2024 VERSAtile Reads. All rights reserved.
This material is protected by copyright, any infringement will be dealt with legal and punitive action.

B) The public IP address that represents one or more inside local IP addresses

C) The IP address of an outside host as it appears to the inside network

D) The public IP address assigned to a host on the outside network

293. Which type of NAT provides a static one-to-one mapping of a local IP address to a global IP address?

A) Static NAT

B) Pooled NAT

C) Port Address Translation (PAT)

D) Dynamic NAT

294. What does Pooled NAT provide?

A) A static one-to-one mapping of a local IP address to a global IP address

B) A dynamic one-to-one mapping of a local IP address to a global IP address

C) A dynamic many-to-one mapping of many local IP addresses to one global IP address

D) A dynamic many-to-many mapping of local IP addresses to global IP addresses

295. What is the primary purpose of Port Address Translation (PAT)?

A) To provide a static one-to-one mapping of a local IP address to a global IP address

B) To provide a dynamic one-to-one mapping of a local IP address to a global IP address

C) To provide a dynamic many-to-one mapping of many local IP addresses to one global IP address

Copyright © 2024 VERSAtile Reads. All rights reserved.
This material is protected by copyright, any infringement will be dealt with legal and punitive action.

D) To provide a dynamic many-to-many mapping of local IP addresses to global IP addresses

296. How does a NAT device identify the specific private IP address for return network traffic in PAT?

A) By using a unique IP address

B) By using a unique port

C) By using a unique MAC address

D) By using a unique VLAN ID

297. Which command is used to configure an interface as an outside interface for NAT?

A) ip nat inside

B) ip nat outside

C) ip nat enable

D) ip nat pool

298. Which command is used to configure an interface as an inside interface for NAT?

A) ip nat inside

B) ip nat outside

C) ip nat enable

D) ip nat pool

299. What is the default timeout period for dynamic NAT translations?

A) 1 hour

B) 12 hours

Copyright © 2024 VERSAtile Reads. All rights reserved.
This material is protected by copyright, any infringement will be dealt with legal and punitive action.

C) 24 hours

D) 48 hours

300. Which command is used to define the global pool of IP addresses in NAT?

A) ip nat inside source list

B) ip nat outside source list

C) ip nat pool

D) ip nat static

301. What does the GRE stand for?

A) Generic Routing Encapsulation

B) General Routing Encapsulation

C) Generic Router Encapsulation

D) General Router Encapsulation

302. What is the primary purpose of GRE tunnels?

A) To encrypt data

B) To compress data

C) To encapsulate and forward packets over an IP-based network

D) To authenticate data

303. Which protocol is typically used to create VPNs by tunneling traffic?

A) GRE

B) OSPF

C) BGP

Copyright © 2024 VERSAtile Reads. All rights reserved.

This material is protected by copyright, any infringement will be dealt with legal and punitive action. 91

D) EIGRP

304. What happens to a packet when it is encapsulated in a GRE tunnel?

A) It is encrypted

B) It is compressed

C) New header information is added

D) The payload is removed

305. What is the term for removing GRE headers at the remote endpoint?

A) De-encapsulation

B) Encapsulation

C) Decapsulation

D) Header stripping

306. What common issue can occur when using a routing protocol on a network tunnel?

A) Packet loss

B) High latency

C) Recursive routing

D) Bandwidth throttling

307. How does a router detect recursive routing?

A) By monitoring traffic patterns

B) By generating a Syslog message

C) By checking routing tables

D) By inspecting packet headers

Copyright © 2024 VERSAtile Reads. All rights reserved.

This material is protected by copyright, any infringement will be dealt with legal and punitive action.

VERSAtile Reads

308. What happens to the tunnel when recursive routing is detected?

A) The tunnel is brought down

B) The tunnel bandwidth is reduced

C) The tunnel is rerouted

D) The tunnel is encrypted

309. What does the IP authentication header provide?

A) Data confidentiality

B) Data integrity

C) Data compression

D) Data fragmentation

310. What is the protocol number for the IP authentication header?

A) 50

B) 51

C) 52

D) 53

311. What does ESP stand for in networking?

A) Encapsulating Security Payload

B) Encryption Security Protocol

C) Encapsulation Secure Protocol

D) Encryption Secure Payload

312. What is a primary feature of ESP?

Copyright © 2024 VERSAtile Reads. All rights reserved.
This material is protected by copyright, any infringement will be dealt with legal and punitive action.

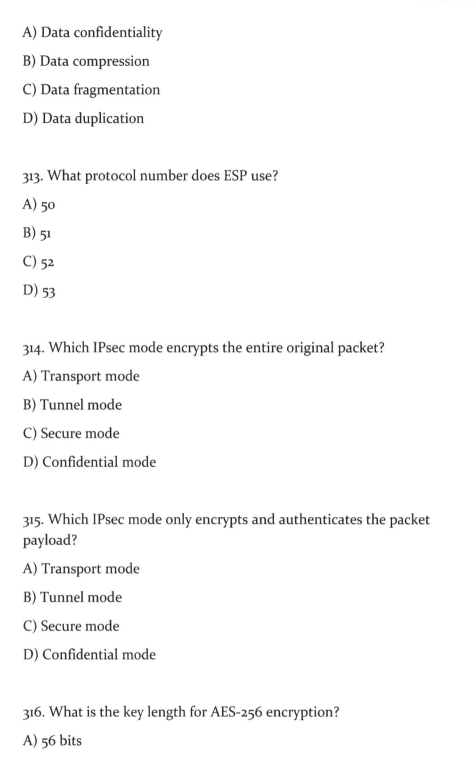

A) Data confidentiality

B) Data compression

C) Data fragmentation

D) Data duplication

313. What protocol number does ESP use?

A) 50

B) 51

C) 52

D) 53

314. Which IPsec mode encrypts the entire original packet?

A) Transport mode

B) Tunnel mode

C) Secure mode

D) Confidential mode

315. Which IPsec mode only encrypts and authenticates the packet payload?

A) Transport mode

B) Tunnel mode

C) Secure mode

D) Confidential mode

316. What is the key length for AES-256 encryption?

A) 56 bits

Copyright © 2024 VERSAtile Reads. All rights reserved.
This material is protected by copyright, any infringement will be dealt with legal and punitive action.

B) 128 bits

C) 192 bits

D) 256 bits

317. What does DES stand for in encryption?

A) Data Encryption Standard

B) Data Encoding Standard

C) Data Encryption Scheme

D) Data Encoding Scheme

318. What is a characteristic of DES encryption?

A) It is very secure

B) It is very weak

C) It uses asymmetric keys

D) It is a hashing algorithm

319. What does 3DES stand for?

A) Triple Data Encryption Standard

B) Threefold Data Encryption Standard

C) Tertiary Data Encryption Standard

D) Triple Data Encoding Standard

320. Which encryption algorithm is recommended over DES and 3DES?

A) MD5

B) SHA

C) AES

Copyright © 2024 VERSAtile Reads. All rights reserved.

This material is protected by copyright, any infringement will be dealt with legal and punitive action.

D) RSA

321. What is the key length of SHA-1?

A) 128 bits

B) 160 bits

C) 192 bits

D) 256 bits

322. What is the function of MD5 in networking?

A) Data encryption

B) Data authentication

C) Data compression

D) Data fragmentation

323. Which encryption algorithm provides better protection against Man-in-the-Middle (MitM) attacks compared to MD5?

A) DES

B) 3DES

C) SHA

D) AES

324. What is Diffie-Hellman used for?

A) Encrypting data

B) Exchanging keys

C) Compressing data

D) Hashing data

Copyright © 2024 VERSAtile Reads. All rights reserved.
This material is protected by copyright, any infringement will be dealt with legal and punitive action.

325. What does a DH group refer to?

A) The length of the key used for encryption

B) The length of the key used for hashing

C) The length of the key used for a DH key exchange

D) The length of the key used for data compression

326. Which DH groups are recommended by Cisco?

A) Groups 1, 2, and 5

B) Groups 14 and higher

C) Groups 1, 3, and 5

D) Groups 10 and 12

327. What are RSA signatures used for?

A) Encrypting data

B) Authenticating peers

C) Compressing data

D) Hashing data

328. What is the purpose of a pre-shared key in IPsec?

A) To encrypt data

B) To compress data

C) To mutually authenticate peers

D) To hash data

Copyright © 2024 VERSAtile Reads. All rights reserved.

This material is protected by copyright, any infringement will be dealt with legal and punitive action.

329. How does NAT help when a company buys another company with overlapping networks?

A) By encrypting the traffic

B) By providing static IP addresses

C) By translating overlapping IP addresses

D) By compressing the traffic

330. What is a major drawback of static NAT?

A) It is less secure

B) It requires many configuration entries

C) It is difficult to implement

D) It uses too much bandwidth

331. In pooled NAT, what happens to the global IP address after the timeout period expires?

A) It is permanently assigned to the local IP address

B) It is returned to the pool for reuse

C) It is discarded

D) It is encrypted

332. What feature of Cisco SD-WAN allows for automatic selection of the best path based on performance metrics?

A) OSPF

B) BGP

C) Dynamic Multipoint VPN (DMVPN)

D) Application-Aware Routing

Copyright © 2024 VERSAtile Reads. All rights reserved.
This material is protected by copyright, any infringement will be dealt with legal and punitive action.

333. Which term describes the unique identifier used by a NAT device to track return traffic in PAT?

A) IP address

B) MAC address

C) Port

D) VLAN ID

334. What is the role of the ip nat inside command?

A) To configure the inside interface for NAT

B) To configure the outside interface for NAT

C) To enable NAT on a device

D) To disable NAT on a device

335. What does the command ip nat pool do?

A) Configures an inside interface for NAT

B) Configures an outside interface for NAT

C) Defines the global pool of IP addresses for NAT

D) Enables NAT on a device

336. Which type of NAT is suitable for dynamically assigning global IP addresses on an as-needed basis?

A) Static NAT

B) Pooled NAT

C) Port Address Translation (PAT)

D) Dynamic NAT

337. What does GRE encapsulation involve?

Copyright © 2024 VERSAtile Reads. All rights reserved.

This material is protected by copyright, any infringement will be dealt with legal and punitive action.

A) Adding new header information to the packet

B) Encrypting the packet

C) Compressing the packet

D) Fragmenting the packet

338. What is a key feature of IPsec tunnel mode?

A) Encrypts only the packet payload

B) Encrypts the entire original packet

C) Compresses the packet

D) Fragments the packet

339. What does the command ip nat inside source list acl pool nat-pool-name do?

A) Configures the inside interface for NAT

B) Configures the outside interface for NAT

C) Defines the global pool of IP addresses for NAT

D) Configures inside pooled NAT

340. What problem can recursive routing cause in a network tunnel?

A) It can cause the tunnel to go down repeatedly

B) It can reduce the tunnel bandwidth

C) It can increase the tunnel latency

D) It can encrypt the tunnel traffic

341. What does the IPsec ESP protocol provide that the authentication header does not?

A) Data integrity

Copyright © 2024 VERSAtile Reads. All rights reserved.
This material is protected by copyright, any infringement will be dealt with legal and punitive action.

B) Data confidentiality

C) Data authentication

D) Data compression

342. Which IPsec encryption algorithm supports key lengths of 128, 192, or 256 bits?

A) DES

B) 3DES

C) AES

D) RSA

343. What is the main function of Internet Key Exchange (IKE)?

A) To manage IP addresses

B) To establish security associations (SAs)

C) To route traffic efficiently

D) To encrypt data packets

344. Which RFC specifies IKEv2?

A) RFC 2409

B) RFC 7296

C) RFC 4301

D) RFC 1918

345. What port does ISAKMP use for communication between peers?

A) TCP 80

B) UDP 500

Copyright © 2024 VERSAtile Reads. All rights reserved.

This material is protected by copyright, any infringement will be dealt with legal and punitive action. 101

C) TCP 443

D) UDP 53

346. Which of the following is NOT a characteristic of IKEv2?

A) Supports EAP

B) Anti-DoS capabilities

C) Needs fewer messages to establish an IPsec SA

D) Incompatible with IKEv1

347. How many messages are exchanged in IKEv1's Main Mode during Phase 1 negotiation?

A) Three

B) Four

C) Six

D) Nine

348. In IKEv1, what is the purpose of Phase 2?

A) To establish bidirectional ISAKMP SAs

B) To establish unidirectional IPsec SAs

C) To authenticate users

D) To encrypt data traffic

349. Which mode in IKEv1 is faster but less secure, and exposes the identities of the peers?

A) Main Mode

B) Aggressive Mode

C) Quick Mode

Copyright © 2024 VERSAtile Reads. All rights reserved.

This material is protected by copyright, any infringement will be dealt with legal and punitive action. 102

D) Diffie-Hellman Mode

350. What is the primary benefit of Perfect Forward Secrecy (PFS) in IKE Phase 2?

A) Faster key exchange

B) Lower CPU usage

C) Greater resistance to crypto attacks

D) Simplified SA negotiation

Copyright © 2024 VERSAtile Reads. All rights reserved.

This material is protected by copyright, any infringement will be dealt with legal and punitive action. 103

Answers

1. D) Layer 7

Explanation: Layer 7 of the OSI (Open Systems Interconnection) model, also known as the Application layer, is where applications generate data. This layer interacts directly with software applications and represents the highest level in the OSI model. It provides network services directly to end-user applications such as web browsers, email clients, and file transfer applications.

2. B) Bridges

Explanation: Bridges are the first Layer 2 devices historically used to segment networks and manage traffic.

3. B) Layer 2

Explanation: Layer 2 (Data Link Layer) handles physical addressing, such as MAC addresses, which is beneath the IP protocol stack at Layer 3.

4. D) Repeating traffic out of every port

Explanation: A network hub repeats incoming traffic out of all ports, regardless of the destination.

5. B) CSMA/CD

Explanation: Ethernet uses Carrier Sense Multiple Access with Collision Detection (CSMA/CD) to manage communication within a collision domain.

6. A) MAC address table

Copyright © 2024 VERSAtile Reads. All rights reserved.

This material is protected by copyright, any infringement will be dealt with legal and punitive action.

Explanation: Switches use a MAC address table to forward frames only to the appropriate port associated with the destination MAC address.

7. D) 48 bits

Explanation: A MAC address is a 48-bit identifier assigned to network interfaces for communications on the physical network segment.

8. B) FF:FF:FF:FF:FF

Explanation: The MAC address FF:FF:FF:FF:FF

is reserved for broadcast messages to all devices on a network segment.

9. A) VLANs

Explanation: Virtual LANs (VLANs) are used to create separate broadcast domains on the same physical network switch.

10. B) 802.1Q

Explanation: The IEEE 802.1Q standard defines VLAN tagging used to segregate network traffic.

11. C) 12 bits

Explanation: The VLAN identifier (VID) in the 802.1Q standard is 12 bits, allowing for 4096 unique VLANs.

12. A) VLAN 0

Explanation: VLAN 0 is reserved for priority-tagged frames in 802.1P and cannot be modified or deleted.

13. B) VLAN 1

Copyright © 2024 VERSAtile Reads. All rights reserved.

This material is protected by copyright, any infringement will be dealt with legal and punitive action.

Explanation: VLAN 1 is the default VLAN on Cisco Catalyst switches.

14. B) Access port

Explanation: An access port is assigned to a single VLAN and carries traffic for that VLAN to and from the connected device.

15. A) switchport mode access

Explanation: The command switchport mode access is used to configure a port as an access port manually.

16. C) Multiple

Explanation: Trunk ports can carry traffic for multiple VLANs by tagging frames with VLAN IDs.

17. A) switchport trunk allowed vlan

Explanation: The command switchport trunk allowed vlan specifies which VLANs are allowed on the trunk.

18. A) VLAN 1

Explanation: VLAN 1 is the default native VLAN on trunk ports.

19. D) Handle untagged traffic

Explanation: The native VLAN handles untagged traffic on a trunk port.

20. B) switchport trunk allowed add vlan-ids

Explanation: The command switchport trunk allowed add vlan-ids adds VLANs to the list of those allowed on a trunk.

Copyright © 2024 VERSAtile Reads. All rights reserved.

This material is protected by copyright, any infringement will be dealt with legal and punitive action.

VERSAtile Reads

21. D) show interfaces trunk

Explanation: The command show interfaces trunk provides information about trunk ports, including associated VLANs and status.

22. C) Section 3

Explanation: Section 3 of the show interfaces trunk command output displays the list of VLANs allowed on the trunk port.

23. D) Control

Explanation: The native VLAN on trunk ports is associated with controlling traffic, and handling untagged frames.

24. A) Higher utilization of switch ports

Explanation: VLANs do not inherently lead to higher utilization of switch ports; they mainly reduce broadcast domains, improve security, and manage traffic more effectively.

25. C) ip default-network

Explanation: The ip default-network command in EIGRP is used to indicate a network as the default network. EIGRP will then advertise this network as the default route to its neighbors. This is different from OSPF, where default-information originate would be used.

26. B) Carrier Sense Multiple Access/Collision Detect

Explanation: CSMA/CD stands for Carrier Sense Multiple Access with Collision Detection, used in Ethernet networks to manage data transmission.

Copyright © 2024 VERSAtile Reads. All rights reserved.

This material is protected by copyright, any infringement will be dealt with legal and punitive action.

27. C) To manage network traffic

Explanation: CSMA/CD helps manage network traffic by detecting collisions and retransmitting data after a random back-off period.

28. B) MAC

Explanation: The MAC (Media Access Control) protocol is used for Layer 2 addressing in Ethernet networks.

29. B) Based on MAC addresses

Explanation: Switches forward network traffic based on MAC addresses to ensure efficient data delivery.

30. A) Segmenting broadcast domains

Explanation: Network bridges segment broadcast domains by filtering traffic and forwarding it to specific segments.

31. C) Forward traffic based on MAC addresses

Explanation: Layer 2 switches use MAC addresses to make forwarding decisions within the same network segment.

32. B) Switch

Explanation: A switch operates at the Data Link layer (Layer 2) of the OSI model.

33. C) Router

Explanation: Routers determine the best path for data packets to reach their destination across different networks.

Copyright © 2024 VERSAtile Reads. All rights reserved.
This material is protected by copyright, any infringement will be dealt with legal and punitive action.

VERSAtile Reads

34. C) Session layer

Explanation: The Session layer (Layer 5) is responsible for establishing, maintaining, and terminating connections between applications.

35. D) IP

Explanation: The Internet Protocol (IP) operates at the Network layer (Layer 3) of the OSI model.

36. D) Routes data packets to their destinations

Explanation: The Network layer is responsible for routing data packets to their destination based on logical addressing.

37. A) Transmission Control Protocol

Explanation: TCP stands for Transmission Control Protocol, which ensures reliable communication between devices.

38. C) TCP

Explanation: TCP provides reliable, connection-oriented communication at the Transport layer.

39. B) Data link layer (Layer 2)

Explanation: Switches primarily operate at the Data Link layer of the OSI model.

40. D) Provides error detection and correction mechanisms

Explanation: The Data Link layer is responsible for error detection and correction in data transmission.

Copyright © 2024 VERSAtile Reads. All rights reserved.
This material is protected by copyright, any infringement will be dealt with legal and punitive action.

41. C) Manages data traffic between applications running on different hosts

Explanation: The Transport layer manages end-to-end data traffic between applications on different hosts.

42. A) Provides encryption and decryption services for secure data transmission

Explanation: The Presentation layer handles data encryption, decryption, and format translation.

43. D) Presentation layer

Explanation: The Presentation layer converts data into a suitable format for transmission over the network.

44. D) Allows access to network services for user applications

Explanation: The Application layer provides network services to end-user applications.

45. C) It is a proprietary model developed by Cisco Systems.

Explanation: The OSI model is not proprietary to Cisco; it is a standard model developed by the ISO.

46. A) It simplifies the design and implementation of complex networking systems.

Explanation: A layered approach like the OSI model simplifies networking system design and implementation.

47. B) Transport layer

Explanation: The Transport layer is responsible for error detection and recovery to ensure reliable data transmission.

Copyright © 2024 VERSAtile Reads. All rights reserved.
This material is protected by copyright, any infringement will be dealt with legal and punitive action. 110

VERSAtile Reads

48. B) Network layer

Explanation: The Network layer handles logical addressing and routing of data packets.

49. D) Application layer

Explanation: The Application layer provides a common interface for applications to access network services.

50. B) To prevent unknown unicast flooding

Explanation: A static MAC address entry prevents unknown unicast flooding by ensuring that the switch knows the specific port for the MAC address.

51. A) mac address-table static

Explanation: This command adds a static entry to the MAC address table, associating a MAC address with a specific switch port or instructing the switch to drop traffic from that MAC address.

52. C) Content Addressable Memory (CAM)

Explanation: The MAC address table resides in Content Addressable Memory (CAM), which is optimized for fast lookups.

53. C) By providing a binary result

Explanation: CAM provides results for queries by comparing input data and returning a binary result, indicating a match or mismatch.

54. C) clear mac address-table dynamic

Copyright © 2024 VERSAtile Reads. All rights reserved.

This material is protected by copyright, any infringement will be dealt with legal and punitive action. **111**

Explanation: This command flushes the dynamic entries from the MAC address table across the entire switch.

55. B) Switch port status

Explanation: The show interfaces interface-id switchport command provides detailed status information about a specific switch port, including its operational mode and VLAN assignments.

56. D) Trunk

Explanation: The operational mode of port Gi1/0/5 is Trunk, which means it can carry traffic for multiple VLANs.

57. C) Status

Explanation: The "Status" field in the show interface status command output indicates whether a link is connected or not.

58. C) As trunk

Explanation: Trunk links are represented as "trunk" in the show interface status output.

59. B) To map Layer 3 IP addresses to Layer 2 MAC addresses

Explanation: The ARP table maps Layer 3 IP addresses to Layer 2 MAC addresses, facilitating the communication between devices on a local network.

60. B) By sending a unicast response

Explanation: When a device sends out an ARP request to resolve an IP address to a MAC address, it expects an ARP reply from the device with that IP address. Upon receiving the ARP reply, which contains the MAC address

Copyright © 2024 VERSAtile Reads. All rights reserved.
This material is protected by copyright, any infringement will be dealt with legal and punitive action.

corresponding to the IP address in question, the device updates its local ARP table. This update is done by sending a unicast response directly to the device that sent the ARP reply. This ensures that the ARP table of the receiving device is updated with the correct MAC address mapping for future communication with that IP address.

61. D) When devices are on different subnets

Explanation: Packets must be routed when devices are on different subnets, requiring traversal through a router.

62. A) To identify its next-hop IP address

Explanation: The source device checks its local routing table to identify the next-hop IP address for forwarding packets to a different network.

63. D) Floating routes

Explanation: Floating routes in the routing table are learned from a default gateway and act as backup routes with higher administrative distances.

64. B) Destination IP address

Explanation: The source device needs the destination IP address to forward packets to a different network.

65. C) Source MAC address

Explanation: The next router modifies the Source MAC address in the packet to its own MAC address before forwarding it to the next hop.

66. B) Changing MAC addresses

Explanation: Layer 2 addressing rewrite involves changing the MAC addresses as packets traverse through different network segments.

Copyright © 2024 VERSAtile Reads. All rights reserved.

This material is protected by copyright, any infringement will be dealt with legal and punitive action.

67. A) show ip arp

Explanation: The show ip arp command displays the ARP table, showing mappings between IP addresses and MAC addresses.

68. C) To allow multiple IPv4 networks on the same interface

Explanation: Adding a secondary IPv4 address to an interface allows it to handle traffic for multiple IPv4 networks.

69. A) Using the command "ipv6 address"

Explanation: IPv6 addresses are assigned to an interface using the ipv6 address command.

70. A) Zero

Explanation: The administrative distance (AD) of connected routes is zero, indicating the highest priority.

71. D) Default-gateway route

Explanation: A default-gateway route entry provides a simplified static default route, directing traffic to a specified gateway when no other route is found.

72. A) By using ARP

Explanation: A device uses ARP to determine the destination MAC address when forwarding packets to a different network.

73. C) Next-hop IP address

Copyright © 2024 VERSAtile Reads. All rights reserved.

This material is protected by copyright, any infringement will be dealt with legal and punitive action. 114

Explanation: The source device identifies the next-hop IP address from its local routing table for forwarding packets.

74. A) clear mac address-table dynamic

Explanation: This command clears the MAC address table for the entire switch, removing dynamic entries.

75. C) To view switch port status

Explanation: The show interfaces switchport command provides detailed status information about switch ports, including their configurations and operational statuses.

76. A) The VLAN assigned to the access port

Explanation: The "Access Mode VLAN" field indicates the VLAN that is assigned to the access port in access mode.

77. D) Port connectivity

Explanation: The "Status" field in the show interface status command indicates whether a port is connected or not.

78. C) Layer 3 IP addresses to Layer 2 MAC addresses

Explanation: The ARP table maps Layer 3 IP addresses to Layer 2 MAC addresses, allowing for proper addressing on a local network.

79. B) Supports multivendor interoperability

Explanation: Site-to-site IPsec VPNs are versatile because they support multivendor interoperability, allowing different vendors' devices to communicate securely.

Copyright © 2024 VERSAtile Reads. All rights reserved.

This material is protected by copyright, any infringement will be dealt with legal and punitive action. 115

80. C) Cisco Dynamic Multipoint VPN (DMVPN)

Explanation: Cisco DMVPN simplifies VPN configuration by using a combination of multipoint GRE (mGRE) tunnels, IPsec, and NHRP.

81. C) mGRE, IPsec, and NHRP

Explanation: DMVPN uses multipoint GRE (mGRE) tunnels, IPsec for security, and Next Hop Resolution Protocol (NHRP) to simplify and dynamically manage VPN configurations.

82. B) Service provider MPLS networks

Explanation: Cisco Group Encrypted Transport VPN (GET VPN) is designed for enterprises to build any-to-any tunnel-less VPNs over service provider MPLS networks or private WANs.

83. A) Creates any-to-any tunnel-less VPNs

Explanation: GET VPN creates any-to-any tunnel-less VPNs, which means the original IP header is used, and it operates without creating additional tunnels.

84. B) HIPAA, Sarbanes-Oxley, PCI DSS, GLBA

Explanation: Cisco GET VPN helps address regulatory compliance guidelines such as HIPAA, Sarbanes-Oxley, PCI DSS, and GLBA by providing secure encryption over private networks.

85. C) Combines multiple VPN topologies

Explanation: Cisco FlexVPN is a highly flexible VPN solution that combines various VPN technologies into a single, unified platform. It supports a wide range of VPN topologies, including site-to-site, remote access, hub-and-

Copyright © 2024 VERSAtile Reads. All rights reserved.
This material is protected by copyright, any infringement will be dealt with legal and punitive action.

spoke, and dynamic multipoint VPN (DMVPN). This flexibility allows organizations to deploy different types of VPNs according to their specific needs while managing them centrally through a single platform.

86. D) Remote VPN Access

Explanation: Remote VPN access allows users to securely connect to a corporate network from remote locations, supported by technologies like FlexVPN and ASA firewalls.

87. B) To provide encryption and authentication for GRE tunnels

Explanation: GRE over IPsec is used to provide encryption and authentication for GRE tunnels. While GRE allows the encapsulation of various network protocols, it lacks security features. Combining it with IPsec secures the encapsulated traffic, ensuring data confidentiality and integrity. This makes GRE over IPsec ideal for securely transmitting diverse network traffic over insecure networks.

88. C) Consumes excessive TCAM space

Explanation: Crypto maps have the major limitation of consuming excessive TCAM (Ternary Content Addressable Memory) space. TCAM is finite hardware memory used for storing access control entries (ACEs) and other forwarding information in networking devices like routers and switches. Using crypto maps extensively can lead to the exhaustion of TCAM resources, impacting the performance and scalability of the device.

89. A) ip access-list extended

Explanation: In IPsec configuration, the ip access-list extended command is used to classify VPN traffic. This command is used to create an extended access control list (ACL) that specifies the traffic to be protected by IPsec.

90. B) DES and MD5

Copyright © 2024 VERSAtile Reads. All rights reserved.

This material is protected by copyright, any infringement will be dealt with legal and punitive action.

Explanation: The encryption algorithms DES (Data Encryption Standard) and MD5 (Message Digest Algorithm 5) are no longer recommended for ISAKMP (Internet Security Association and Key Management Protocol) policy due to their vulnerabilities and weaknesses in providing secure communication. It is recommended to use stronger encryption algorithms like AES (Advanced Encryption Standard) instead.

91. B) To configure the pre-shared key (PSK)

Explanation: The purpose of the crypto isakmp key command is to configure the pre-shared key (PSK) used for authentication between IPsec peers during the IKE (Internet Key Exchange) negotiation process.

92. C) AES

Explanation: AES (Advanced Encryption Standard) is recommended over DES (Data Encryption Standard) and 3DES (Triple Data Encryption Standard) for ISAKMP encryption algorithm due to its stronger security properties and better performance.

93. C) To specify transform sets for IPsec negotiation

Explanation: An IPsec profile is used to specify transform sets for IPsec negotiation. Transform sets define the combination of security protocols, algorithms, and other parameters used for protecting IPsec traffic between peers.

94. B) Using the 'tunnel protection ipsec profile' command

Explanation: An IPsec profile is applied to a tunnel interface using the tunnel protection ipsec profile command. This command associates the configured IPsec profile with the tunnel interface, enabling IPsec protection for the traffic traversing through that interface.

95. B) UDP

Copyright © 2024 VERSAtile Reads. All rights reserved.
This material is protected by copyright, any infringement will be dealt with legal and punitive action.

Explanation: LISP (Location/ID Separation Protocol) improves load sharing by preventing polarization for UDP (User Datagram Protocol) traffic. By using a tactically selected source port in the UDP header, LISP ensures that traffic from one LISP site to another takes different paths, enhancing load sharing and avoiding traffic polarization issues.

96. A) Limited VLAN ID space

Explanation: Traditional Layer 2 networks face issues with server virtualization because the 12-bit VLAN ID yields only 4000 VLANs, which are insufficient for the increased number of VMs and containers that need unique VLANs.

97. C) The default UDP destination port used by Linux is 8472.

Explanation: The default UDP destination port used by Linux is 8472 because when VXLAN was first implemented in Linux, the official port had not been assigned by IANA, which later assigned port 4789. To avoid breaking existing deployments, Linux retained port 8472 as the default value.

98. D) 16 million

Explanation: VXLAN uses a 24-bit VXLAN network identifier (VNI), which allows for up to 16 million VXLAN segments, addressing the limitations of traditional VLANs that can only support up to 4000 segments.

99. B) To prevent loops in Layer 2 networks

Explanation: The primary purpose of the Spanning Tree Protocol (STP) is to prevent loops in Layer 2 networks.

100. D) Disconnected

Copyright © 2024 VERSAtile Reads. All rights reserved.

This material is protected by copyright, any infringement will be dealt with legal and punitive action.

Explanation: "Disconnected" is not a port state in the 802.1D STP protocol; the valid states are Disabled, Listening, Learning, and Forwarding.

101. A) To forward traffic toward the root bridge

Explanation: The Root Port (RP) is the port on a switch that is closest to the root bridge in terms of path cost. It forwards traffic towards the root bridge.

102. D) The port is not forwarding traffic to prevent loops.

Explanation: In the Blocking state, the port does not forward traffic to prevent Layer 2 loops in the network.

103. D) 30 seconds

Explanation: It typically takes 30 seconds for a port to transition to the Forwarding state in 802.1D STP using default timers, with 15 seconds each in the Listening and Learning states.

104. B) Routing table

Explanation: The routing table is not related to STP. Key terms related to STP include Root bridge, BPDU, and Root path cost.

105. A) The maximum age of a BPDU packet

Explanation: The Max Age timer determines how long a BPDU is retained before being discarded if no new BPDU is received.

106. A) Root port (RP)

Explanation: The Root Port connects to the root bridge or an upstream switch and is the port with the best path to the root bridge.

Copyright © 2024 VERSAtile Reads. All rights reserved.
This material is protected by copyright, any infringement will be dealt with legal and punitive action. 120

107. B) To identify a hierarchy and notify of topology changes

Explanation: The Bridge Protocol Data Unit (BPDU) is a fundamental message used in Spanning Tree Protocol (STP) and its variants (Rapid Spanning Tree Protocol, MSTP) to establish and maintain loop-free Layer 2 network topology. BPDU frames are exchanged between switches to detect loops in the network and elect a root bridge. They also carry information about the network topology, such as bridge IDs, port IDs, and path costs. When there are changes in the network topology (e.g., link failures, new switches added), BPDUs are used to notify other switches so they can adjust their forwarding tables accordingly.

108. A) To improve convergence time in the spanning tree topology

Explanation: RSTP enhances the speed of convergence of the spanning tree topology compared to the original STP.

109. B) To prevent Layer 2 loops

Explanation: The primary purpose of STP is to prevent Layer 2 loops, which can cause broadcast storms and network failures.

110. B) 802.1D

Explanation: The IEEE 802.1D standard originally defined the Spanning Tree Protocol (STP).

111. B) Connects to the root bridge or an upstream switch

Explanation: The Root Port is the port that connects to the root bridge or an upstream switch and has the best path to the root bridge.

112. D) Forwarding

Explanation: In the Forwarding state, the switch port can send and receive all network traffic and BPDUs.

Copyright © 2024 VERSAtile Reads. All rights reserved.

This material is protected by copyright, any infringement will be dealt with legal and punitive action.

113. C) The time before a bridge port saves its BPDU information

Explanation: The Max Age parameter in STP determines the time before the switch discards BPDU information if it doesn't receive a new BPDU.

114. B) Designated port (DP)

Explanation: The Designated Port connects to downstream devices and switches, forwarding traffic away from the root bridge.

115. B) It identifies the VLAN that the BPDU correlates to

Explanation: The System ID Extension is used to identify the VLAN for which the BPDU is relevant.

116. B) RSTP

Explanation: Rapid Spanning Tree Protocol (RSTP) is backward compatible with the IEEE 802.1D standard.

117. A) By selecting the switch with the lowest MAC address

Explanation: STP determines the Root Bridge by selecting the switch with the lowest bridge ID, which includes the lowest MAC address and priority.

118. A) Root port (RP)

Explanation: The Root Port forwards traffic toward the root bridge or an upstream switch.

119. A) To identify the root bridge and root ports

Explanation: Configuration BPDUs are used to identify the root bridge and the roles of ports in the spanning-tree topology.

Copyright © 2024 VERSAtile Reads. All rights reserved.
This material is protected by copyright, any infringement will be dealt with legal and punitive action. **122**

120. A) Listening

Explanation: In the Listening state, a switch port receives BPDUs and sends its own BPDUs but does not forward other network traffic.

121. D) Root path cost

Explanation: STP uses the Root Path Cost to calculate the combined cost for a specific path toward the root switch.

122. A) Broken

Explanation: A Broken port state indicates a major configuration or operational problem on a port.

123. C) By dynamically selecting specific ports to block temporarily

Explanation: STP handles redundant ports by dynamically blocking some ports to prevent loops while allowing traffic on other ports.

124. B) The port modifies the MAC address table with network traffic

Explanation: In the Learning state, the port learns MAC addresses and updates the MAC address table but does not forward traffic yet.

125. C) The lowest system MAC address

Explanation: The preference for a switch to become the root bridge in STP is determined by the lowest bridge ID, which includes the system MAC address and priority.

126. B) To communicate changes in the Layer 2 topology

Copyright © 2024 VERSAtile Reads. All rights reserved.

This material is protected by copyright, any infringement will be dealt with legal and punitive action.

VERSAtile Reads

Explanation: The Topology Change Notification (TCN) BPDU informs other switches about changes in the network topology.

127. D) Forwarding

Explanation: The Forwarding state is the final state in which a switch port can send and receive all network traffic.

128. C) Forward delay

Explanation: The duration of the Learning state in STP is determined by the Forward Delay timer, which is 15 seconds by default.

129. A) PVST

Explanation: Per-VLAN Spanning Tree (PVST) mode ensures a loop-free topology for one VLAN.

130. B) By dynamically blocking specific ports temporarily

Explanation: Spanning Tree Protocol (STP) prevents loops in a network topology by dynamically blocking specific ports temporarily. When switches exchange Bridge Protocol Data Units (BPDUs), they elect a root bridge and determine the best path to reach the root bridge from each switch. To prevent loops, STP identifies and blocks redundant paths by placing certain ports in a blocked state. These ports remain blocked until a network change occurs, such as a link failure, which triggers STP to recalculate and potentially unblock a previously blocked port to restore network connectivity without causing loops.

131. A) The preference for a switch to be the root bridge

Explanation: The System Priority parameter indicates a switch's preference for becoming the root bridge. A lower value has a higher priority.

132. B) Max Age

Copyright © 2024 VERSAtile Reads. All rights reserved.

This material is protected by copyright, any infringement will be dealt with legal and punitive action.

Explanation: The duration of the Blocking state is determined by the Max Age timer.

133. B) Designated port (DP)

Explanation: A Designated Port forwards BPDU frames to other switches and is responsible for forwarding traffic for a specific network segment.

134. A) A collection of routers under a single organization's control

Explanation: An Autonomous System (AS) is a group of IP networks and routers under the control of a single entity that presents a common routing policy to the Internet.

135. B) IGP

Explanation: Interior Gateway Protocol (IGP) is used for routing within an AS.

136. B) To uniquely identify an AS

Explanation: The Autonomous System Number (ASN) uniquely identifies each Autonomous System on the internet.

137. B) 65,535

Explanation: There are 65,535 ASNs available in the original 16-bit ASN range (from 1 to 65,535).

138. C) IANA

Explanation: The Internet Assigned Numbers Authority (IANA) is responsible for assigning public ASNs.

Copyright © 2024 VERSAtile Reads. All rights reserved.

This material is protected by copyright, any infringement will be dealt with legal and punitive action. **125**

139. C) Well-known mandatory

Explanation: Well-known mandatory path attributes must be recognized and propagated by all BGP implementations.

140. B) Routing loops

Explanation: The AS_Path attribute in BGP helps to prevent routing loops by listing the ASes that the route has traversed.

141. A) AFI and SAFI

Explanation: Address Family Identifier (AFI) and Subsequent Address Family Identifier (SAFI) are used in Multi-Protocol BGP (MP-BGP) to support multiple network layer protocols.

142. C) 179

Explanation: BGP (Border Gateway Protocol) communication occurs over TCP port 179. BGP is used to exchange routing information between autonomous systems on the internet, and it relies on this specific port to establish and maintain connections between BGP peers. This ensures the proper routing of data across different networks.

143. B) iBGP

Explanation: Internal BGP (iBGP) sessions are used for communication within the same AS.

144. D) 20

Explanation: The Administrative Distance (AD) of External BGP (eBGP) is 20.

145. C) Idle

Copyright © 2024 VERSAtile Reads. All rights reserved.

This material is protected by copyright, any infringement will be dealt with legal and punitive action.

Explanation: A BGP (Border Gateway Protocol) session starts in the Idle state. This is the initial state when a BGP router is waiting to start the connection process. From Idle, the session progresses through various states such as Connect, Active, and others, before reaching the Established state where actual BGP routing information is exchanged between peers.

146. B) 1

Explanation: The default TTL (Time To Live) value for eBGP (External Border Gateway Protocol) sessions is 1. This low TTL value ensures that eBGP sessions are established only with directly connected peers, enhancing security by preventing the establishment of sessions with remote or unintended devices.

147. B) router bgp

Explanation: The command to initialize BGP in the router configuration is router bgp.

148. A) neighbor ip-address remote-as as-number

Explanation: The command to identify a BGP neighbor is neighbor ip-address remote-as as-number.

149. B) 2

Explanation: The Address Family Identifier (AFI) used for IPv6 is 2.

150. C) 200

Explanation: The default Administrative Distance (AD) of Internal BGP (iBGP) is 200.

151. A) Multi-Protocol Reachable Network Layer Reachability Information

Copyright © 2024 VERSAtile Reads. All rights reserved.

This material is protected by copyright, any infringement will be dealt with legal and punitive action. 127

Explanation: MP_REACH_NLRI stands for Multi-Protocol Reachable Network Layer Reachability Information, which is used in BGP to support multiple network layer protocols.

152. B) It discards the prefix

Explanation: If a BGP router detects its own ASN in the AS_Path attribute, it discards the prefix to prevent routing loops.

153. D) Optional non-transitive

Explanation: Optional non-transitive path attributes are not shared between ASs.

154. A) Full mesh of iBGP peers

Explanation: For iBGP to function properly within an AS, a full mesh of iBGP peers is required unless route reflectors or confederations are used.

155. B) It uses the AS_Path attribute

Explanation: BGP uses the AS_Path attribute to prevent routing loops by identifying the ASs a route has traversed.

156. A) AS_Path

Explanation: AS_Path is a well-known mandatory attribute in BGP that must be recognized and included with all BGP updates.

157. A) BGP has no hop limit by default

Explanation: BGP does not have a hop limit by default, unlike IGPs which typically have a hop count limit.

Copyright © 2024 VERSAtile Reads. All rights reserved.
This material is protected by copyright, any infringement will be dealt with legal and punitive action.

158. A) address-family afi safi

Explanation: The command to initialize the Address Family in BGP is address-family afi safi.

159. B) Finite State Machine (FSM)

Explanation: BGP uses a Finite State Machine (FSM) to manage session states.

160. A) It limits the distance of the BGP session

Explanation: The TTL value in eBGP sessions limits the distance the BGP session can traverse, typically to prevent unwanted connections beyond the immediate neighbors.

161. A) IPv4

Explanation: In the context of BGP (Border Gateway Protocol) and network address families, AFI (Address Family Identifier) = 1 represents the IPv4 address family. This identifier is used to specify that the subsequent information pertains to IPv4 addresses.

162. A) bgp router-id

Explanation: To define a router ID in BGP (Border Gateway Protocol), the command used is bgp router-id. This command is typically followed by the IP address that you want to assign as the BGP router ID.

163. B) Using BGP network statements

Explanation: In BGP (Border Gateway Protocol), prefixes (network routes) are advertised to BGP peers using BGP network statements. These statements are configured under the BGP routing process on the router. Here is a brief **Explanation** of how BGP network statements work:

Copyright © 2024 VERSAtile Reads. All rights reserved.
This material is protected by copyright, any infringement will be dealt with legal and punitive action.

- **BGP Network Statements**: In BGP configuration, you specify which prefixes (networks) should be advertised to BGP neighbors using network statements. These statements match the network address (prefix) you want to advertise.

- **Example**: Suppose you want to advertise the network 192.168.1.0/24 via BGP. You would configure a network statement like this:

```
router bgp 65001
network 192.168.1.0 mask 255.255.255.0
```

This tells BGP to advertise the network 192.168.1.0/24 to its BGP neighbors.

164. B) 110

Explanation: The Administrative Distance (AD) of OSPF (Open Shortest Path First) is indeed 110. This means that if a router receives routing information about a particular network from OSPF, it assigns it an AD of 110. Routers use AD to prioritize routing information from different sources when determining the best path to reach a destination network.

165. C) AS_Path

Explanation: The AS_Path attribute influences BGP route selection by preferring shorter AS paths.

166. B) Well-known discretionary

Explanation: Local_Pref is a well-known discretionary path attribute in BGP.

167. B) eBGP

Explanation: eBGP sessions typically require manual peering configuration between external peers.

Copyright © 2024 VERSAtile Reads. All rights reserved.

This material is protected by copyright, any infringement will be dealt with legal and punitive action.

168. C) The session is fully operational

Explanation: The 'Established' state in a BGP session indicates that the session is fully operational and routes can be exchanged.

169. C) 64,512–65,535

Explanation: The valid private 16-bit ASN range is 64,512–65,535.

170. C) Optional transitive

Explanation: The Community attribute in BGP is classified as optional transitive.

171. A) A BGP message is being sent

Explanation: In the context of BGP (Border Gateway Protocol), the 'OpenSent' state signifies that a BGP message, specifically an OPEN message, is being sent from one BGP speaker (router) to another during the BGP session establishment process.

Here is a brief overview of BGP session establishment:

- Idle state: Initial state where no BGP messages are being exchanged.
- Connect state: Indicates that a TCP connection is being attempted.
- OpenSent state: Occurs after a TCP connection is established, where the router sends an OPEN message to initiate the BGP session.
- OpenConfirm state: The router awaits an OPEN message from the peer to confirm the BGP session parameters.
- Established state: The BGP session is fully established and routing information can be exchanged.

172. A) neighbor ip-address activate

Explanation: The command to activate an address family for a BGP neighbor is neighbor ip-address activate.

Copyright © 2024 VERSAtile Reads. All rights reserved.

This material is protected by copyright, any infringement will be dealt with legal and punitive action.

173. A) It specifies the next router in the path

Explanation: The Next-Hop attribute in BGP specifies the next router to which packets should be forwarded.

174. B) Local_Pref

Explanation: The Local_Pref attribute can be used to control route advertisement and selection within an AS.

175. C) To advertise network prefixes

Explanation: The network command in BGP configuration is used to advertise network prefixes.

176. A) Idle

Explanation: The Idle state in BGP indicates that the session has failed or not yet started.

177. C) To manage BGP session states

Explanation: The Finite State Machine (FSM) in BGP is responsible for managing the states of BGP sessions.

178. C) AS_Path

Explanation: BGP uses the AS_Path attribute to determine the best path when multiple routes are available by preferring shorter AS paths.

179. A) neighbor remote-as

Explanation: The command to specify the remote AS for a BGP neighbor is neighbor remote-as.

Copyright © 2024 VERSAtile Reads. All rights reserved.
This material is protected by copyright, any infringement will be dealt with legal and punitive action.

180. B) AS_Path

Explanation: The AS_Path attribute in BGP prevents loops by listing the ASs traversed.

181. B) 64

Explanation: The default TTL value for iBGP sessions is 64.

182. A) Sets the router ID for BGP

Explanation: The command bgp router-id router-id is used in BGP (Border Gateway Protocol) configuration to specify the router ID for the BGP process on a router. The router ID is a unique identifier used by BGP to identify itself to other BGP routers in the network. It is essential for BGP operations, including path selection and establishing BGP neighbor relationships. This command does not specify BGP neighbors, activate address families, or define network prefixes; those tasks are handled by other BGP configuration commands.

183. B) eBGP

Explanation: eBGP (External BGP) is the BGP session type that has a default Administrative Distance (AD) of 20. Administrative Distance (AD) is a measure used by routers to prioritize information received from different routing protocols or sources. eBGP sessions typically occur between routers in different Autonomous Systems (ASes), and the AD of 20 reflects the preference given to routes learned from external sources, such as neighboring ASes.

184. A) Using multiple service providers for redundancy

Explanation: BGP multi-homing involves using multiple service providers to ensure redundancy and availability.

Copyright © 2024 VERSAtile Reads. All rights reserved.

This material is protected by copyright, any infringement will be dealt with legal and punitive action.

185. B) Advertise only the best path

Explanation: By default, BGP advertises only the best path to its neighbors.

186. C) Next Hop

Explanation: The Next Hop attribute in BGP specifies the IP address that packets should be forwarded to in order to reach a destination network. This attribute is crucial for BGP routers to determine the next hop router for a particular route. The Next Hop address can be either the IP address of the BGP neighbor router or a different IP address if the route is learned from an external BGP neighbor.

187. C) To minimize cost and maximize circuit availability

Explanation: Organizations may use different service providers for each circuit to minimize cost and maximize circuit availability.

188. B) Multicast

Explanation: In IPv6, multicast addresses are used for one-to-many communication, allowing a single packet to be delivered to multiple destinations within a specified group. This is useful for services like video streaming and routing protocol updates.

189. D) Cisco DNA Center

Explanation: Cisco DNA Center is a centralized management platform that uses automation to deploy, configure, monitor, and manage network devices in a Cisco network. It provides a single interface for network management tasks and supports intent-based networking principles.

190. B) By configuring outbound route filtering at each branch site

Explanation: To avoid transit routing, outbound route filtering can be configured at each branch site.

Copyright © 2024 VERSAtile Reads. All rights reserved.

This material is protected by copyright, any infringement will be dealt with legal and punitive action.

191. C) Unpredictable and nondeterministic routing patterns

Explanation: If transit routers' circuits become oversaturated, it can lead to unpredictable and nondeterministic routing patterns.

192. C) To provide basic firewall functionality

Explanation: Access Control Lists (ACLs) in routing protocols provide basic firewall functionality by filtering traffic.

193. B) Deny

Explanation: The default action for packets that do not match any ACE (Access Control Entry) in an ACL is to deny them.

194. B) They use numbered entries 1–99 or 1300–1999

Explanation: Standard ACLs use numbered entries from 1 to 99 or 1300 to 1999.

195. B) 0.0.0.0 0.0.0.0

Explanation: The 'any' keyword in an ACL replaces the IP address 0.0.0.0 0.0.0.0, indicating any IP address.

196. A) Prefix lists use high-order bit patterns for matching

Explanation: Prefix lists are used to match prefixes based on high-order bit patterns and are generally more efficient for large scale route filtering than ACLs.

197. C) Sequence number

Copyright © 2024 VERSAtile Reads. All rights reserved.

This material is protected by copyright, any infringement will be dealt with legal and punitive action.

Explanation: The sequence number in a route map dictates the order in which the entries are processed.

198. B) Permit

Explanation: If no processing action is specified in a route map, the default action is to permit.

199. A) Oversaturated circuits

Explanation: Improper transit routing design can lead to oversaturated circuits, affecting network performance.

200. C) Resource Reservation Protocol (RSVP)

Explanation: RSVP is a protocol used to reserve bandwidth across a network to ensure a minimum level of service for critical applications. Traffic Shaping and Policing are used to control traffic rates, while WFQ is a queuing mechanism to ensure fair bandwidth distribution among different traffic flows.

201. B) To prefer routing through MPLS SP2

Explanation: Setting a higher local preference for MPLS SP2 in branch transit routing ensures that routes received from MPLS SP2 are preferred over routes from other service providers. This helps in directing traffic through the desired provider, optimizing network performance, and potentially reducing costs associated with utilizing specific service providers.

202. D) Optional action

Explanation: In a route map, the optional action component allows for modification, addition, or removal of route characteristics. These actions can include setting attributes like local preference, metric, or next-hop,

Copyright © 2024 VERSAtile Reads. All rights reserved.

This material is protected by copyright, any infringement will be dealt with legal and punitive action.

providing flexibility in manipulating routing decisions based on specific conditions.

203. B) By allowing routers to act as transit routers

Explanation: Routing patterns can become unpredictable in a multi-homed design if routers are allowed to act as transit routers. When routers forward traffic not destined for their networks, it can lead to suboptimal routing, increased network complexity, and potential congestion issues.

204. C) The length or mask length

Explanation: A high-order bit pattern in a prefix list represents the length or mask length of the IP address. Prefix lists use these patterns to match specific prefixes or address ranges based on their lengths, allowing for precise control over route filtering and selection.

205. A) They are easier to manage and remember

Explanation: Named ACLs are generally preferred because they are easier to manage and remember compared to numbered ACLs. With named ACLs, administrators can assign descriptive names to ACL entries, making it simpler to understand and maintain network access control policies.

206. B) To modify routing policies on a per-neighbor basis

Explanation: The main reason for using route maps in BGP is to modify routing policies on a per-neighbor basis. Route maps allow BGP administrators to control route advertisement, filtering, and manipulation based on specific criteria, such as neighbor AS number, prefix matching, or route attributes.

207. A) It is mandatory to specify

Copyright © 2024 VERSAtile Reads. All rights reserved.

This material is protected by copyright, any infringement will be dealt with legal and punitive action.

VERSAtile Reads

Explanation: A sequence number is mandatory to specify in a route map statement. It dictates the processing order of route map entries and helps ensure that routing policies are applied in the intended sequence.

208. A) Standard ACL

Explanation: Standard ACLs define packets based solely on the source network. They typically filter traffic based on the source IP address and are used for basic access control decisions.

209. B) Stop processing and take the appropriate action

Explanation: When a match is found in an ACL, processing stops, and the ACL takes the appropriate action specified in the matched Access Control Entry (ACE), such as permitting or denying the packet.

210. C) The sequence number increments by 10 automatically

Explanation: If a sequence number is not provided in a route map statement, the sequence number automatically increments by 10. This default behavior ensures that each route map statement has a unique sequence number by default.

211. B) It enhances redundancy and optimization

Explanation: Using multiple service providers in BGP enhances redundancy and optimization by providing alternative paths for traffic in case of failures or congestion. It allows for load balancing, improved performance, and increased resilience against network outages.

212. B) It can lead to oversaturated circuits

Explanation: Transit routing in branch sites can lead to oversaturated circuits if traffic volumes exceed the capacity of network links. This can result in congestion, increased latency, and reduced network performance.

Copyright © 2024 VERSAtile Reads. All rights reserved.

This material is protected by copyright, any infringement will be dealt with legal and punitive action.

213. B) Deny all traffic

Explanation: The implicit rule at the end of every ACL is to deny all traffic that does not match any preceding ACE. This ensures that any traffic not explicitly permitted by the ACL is denied by default.

214. B) By configuring outbound route filtering

Explanation: To prevent a branch router from acting as a transit router, outbound route filtering can be configured. This ensures that the router only advertises its routes to external neighbors and does not forward transit traffic intended for other networks.

215. B) To define the bit pattern and length for matching

Explanation: The prefix match specification in a prefix list is used to define the bit pattern and length for matching IP address prefixes. It allows administrators to specify the exact criteria for selecting routes to permit or deny.

216. B) A /32 IP address

Explanation: In an ACL, the host keyword refers to a specific /32 IP address, indicating that the ACL rule applies to traffic destined for that exact IP address.

217. B) Routing patterns become unpredictable

Explanation: If the transit router's circuits become oversaturated, routing patterns can become unpredictable. This can lead to suboptimal routing decisions, increased latency, and potential network instability.

218. D) RTP

Copyright © 2024 VERSAtile Reads. All rights reserved.

This material is protected by copyright, any infringement will be dealt with legal and punitive action.

VERSAtile Reads

Explanation: EIGRP (Enhanced Interior Gateway Routing Protocol) uses the Reliable Transport Protocol (RTP) to send hello packets, updates, and other types of EIGRP messages. RTP ensures reliable delivery of these packets between EIGRP neighbors.

219. A) Providing basic firewall functionality

Explanation: Besides filtering packets, a common use of ACLs is providing basic firewall functionality by controlling access to network resources based on specified criteria, such as source IP address, destination IP address, port numbers, or protocol types.

220. A) By avoiding transit routing

Explanation: Routing patterns can be made predictable in a multi-homed environment by avoiding transit routing. This involves configuring the network to prevent routers from forwarding traffic not destined for their own networks, ensuring that traffic follows predetermined paths.

221. A) To add or modify route characteristics

Explanation: The main function of the conditional matching criteria in a route map is to add or modify route characteristics based on specific conditions. This allows administrators to tailor routing policies and manipulate route attributes to meet network requirements.

222. B) Prefix lists provide more detailed network selection

Explanation: An organization might prefer using prefix lists over ACLs in routing protocols because prefix lists provide more detailed network selection criteria and allow for more granular route filtering and manipulation.

223. D) To modify route attributes

Copyright © 2024 VERSAtile Reads. All rights reserved.

This material is protected by copyright, any infringement will be dealt with legal and punitive action. 140

Explanation: The purpose of the processing action in a route map is to modify route attributes, such as local preference, metric, or next-hop, based on specified conditions. This enables administrators to control routing decisions and tailor routing policies to meet specific network requirements.

224. C) LACP

Explanation: LACP (Link Aggregation Control Protocol), also known as IEEE 802.3ad, is used to combine multiple Ethernet links (port channels) into a single logical link, providing increased bandwidth and redundancy. LACP dynamically negotiates the formation of port channels between network devices, allowing them to work together as a single logical link.

225. D) By avoiding transit routing

Explanation: A network design can accommodate outages effectively by avoiding transit routing. This involves configuring the network to prevent routers from acting as transit routers, ensuring that traffic follows predetermined paths, and minimizing the impact of outages on network performance.

226. D) To match routes based on AS path attributes

Explanation: AS path ACLs in conditional matching are used to match routes based on AS path attributes. They allow administrators to filter or manipulate BGP routes based on the ASNs (Autonomous System Numbers) through which the route has traversed.

227. B) It determines the processing order

Explanation: The sequence number in a route map affects processing by determining the order in which the route map entries are applied. Lower sequence numbers are processed first, followed by higher sequence numbers, allowing administrators to define the order of operations for route map actions.

Copyright © 2024 VERSAtile Reads. All rights reserved.

This material is protected by copyright, any infringement will be dealt with legal and punitive action.

228. B) To prefer routing through MPLS SP2

Explanation: Setting a higher local preference for MPLS SP2 in branch transit routing ensures that routes received from MPLS SP2 are preferred over routes from other service providers. This helps in directing traffic through the desired provider, optimizing network performance, and potentially reducing costs associated with utilizing specific service providers.

229. C) Enhanced redundancy and optimization

Explanation: Using different service providers for each circuit can provide enhanced redundancy and optimization for the network. It allows for load balancing, improved performance, and resilience against failures or congestion in a single provider's network.

230. B) By preventing branch routers from acting as transit routers

Explanation: Outbound route filtering in a multi-homed environment can help prevent branch routers from acting as transit routers. It ensures that routers only advertise their routes to external peers, controlling the flow of traffic and preventing the unintentional forwarding of transit traffic.

231. B) To uniquely identify the router in the OSPF domain

Explanation: The "router-id" command in OSPF is used to set a unique identifier for the router within the OSPF domain. This identifier is crucial for the OSPF routing process and does not need to match the router's IP address.

232. C) Not-So-Stubby Area (NSSA)

Copyright © 2024 VERSAtile Reads. All rights reserved.
This material is protected by copyright, any infringement will be dealt with legal and punitive action.

Explanation: A Not-So-Stubby Area (NSSA) allows the redistribution of external routes (Type 7 LSAs) within the area, which are then translated to Type 5 LSAs by the ABR (Area Border Router) to propagate to other areas. However, Type 5 LSAs from other areas are not propagated within the NSSA, preserving some stub area characteristics.

233. D) clear bgp session ip-address

Explanation: The command clear bgp session ip-address is used to initiate a hard reset of a BGP (Border Gateway Protocol) session with a specific peer identified by its IP address. This command forcibly terminates the BGP session and resets all BGP session parameters, including the TCP connection and all BGP state information associated with that session.

234. C) Invalidates the BGP cache and requests a full advertisement

Explanation: A soft reset in BGP invalidates the BGP cache and requests a full advertisement from the peer. It does not tear down the BGP session or remove BGP routes from the peer.

235. B) clear ip bgp

Explanation: The command clear ip bgp * clears all of a router's BGP sessions simultaneously. It resets all BGP sessions and re-establishes BGP peering with neighboring routers.

236. C) Route refresh

Explanation: Route refresh is the capability that allows a BGP peer to re-advertise prefixes to a requesting router without tearing down the BGP session. It provides a mechanism for updating BGP routing information without the need for a full BGP session reset.

237. C) clear bgp afi safi ip-address soft [in | out]

Copyright © 2024 VERSAtile Reads. All rights reserved.

This material is protected by copyright, any infringement will be dealt with legal and punitive action.

Explanation: The command clear bgp afi safi ip-address soft [in | out] initiates a soft reset for a specific address family in BGP. It resets the BGP session with the specified peer for the specified address family without interrupting the entire BGP session.

238. B) To tag routes and modify BGP routing policy

Explanation: The purpose of BGP communities is to tag routes and modify BGP routing policy. BGP communities are used to group routes and apply specific policies to them, such as controlling route propagation, influencing route selection, or defining route preferences.

239. B) (0-65535):(0-65535)

Explanation: The format of a private BGP community is (0-65535):(0-65535). Private BGP communities are typically used for local communication within an AS and are not propagated outside the AS boundary.

240. D) RFC 4360

Explanation: RFC 4360 expanded BGP communities' capabilities to include an extended format. This RFC introduced the concept of extended communities, which provide additional functionality and flexibility for tagging and manipulating BGP routes.

241. C) No_Export

Explanation: The well-known BGP community No_Export indicates routes that should not be advertised to any BGP peer outside the local AS boundary. It is used to prevent the redistribution of routes to external peers.

242. B) Using the command neighbor ip-address send-community

Explanation: Standard BGP communities are enabled on a neighbor-by-neighbor basis using the command neighbor ip-address send-community.

Copyright © 2024 VERSAtile Reads. All rights reserved.
This material is protected by copyright, any infringement will be dealt with legal and punitive action.

VERSAtile Reads

This command allows BGP neighbors to exchange standard BGP communities along with BGP updates.

243. B) Weight

Explanation: The first step in the BGP best-path selection algorithm is the weight attribute. Weight is a Cisco-specific attribute that is local to the router and is not advertised to other BGP peers. It is used as the first tiebreaker in route selection.

244. A) Local preference

Explanation: The Cisco-defined attribute that is not advertised to other routers in the BGP best-path algorithm is Local preference. Local preference is used to indicate the preference for exiting the AS to the destination network and is an attribute local to the router.

245. B) Local preference

Explanation: The attribute that indicates the preference for exiting the AS to the destination network is Local preference. Local preference is used to influence inbound traffic flow by indicating the preferred exit point from the local AS.

246. D) MED

Explanation: The BGP attribute that is non-transitive and influences traffic flows inbound from a different AS is MED (Multi-Exit Discriminator). MED is used to influence the selection of the best path into an AS and is not propagated beyond neighboring ASs.

247. A) show ip bgp

Copyright © 2024 VERSAtile Reads. All rights reserved.

This material is protected by copyright, any infringement will be dealt with legal and punitive action.

Explanation: The command show ip bgp displays the BGP table for a specific network prefix on a router. It shows detailed information about BGP routes, including their origin, path, next hop, and attributes.

248. B) To provide a path metric in environments with multiple ASs

Explanation: The purpose of the AIGP (Additional Paths Information) metric in BGP is to provide a path metric in environments with multiple ASs. It allows BGP routers to exchange additional path information to aid in route selection.

249. B) CDP

Explanation: CDP (Cisco Discovery Protocol) is a Cisco proprietary protocol used to dynamically discover and manage network devices within a Cisco network. It operates at the data link layer (Layer 2) of the OSI model and allows Cisco devices to learn about neighboring Cisco devices directly connected to them.

250. C) 100

Explanation: In BGP, the default local preference value, if not explicitly configured by the network administrator, is set to 100. Local preference is a BGP attribute used to indicate the preferred exit point from an autonomous system (AS) to reach a specific destination network.

251. C) AS_Path

Explanation: The AS_Path attribute in BGP is used to identify the sequence of autonomous systems (AS) through which a route has traversed. It helps BGP routers identify the shortest path to a destination by examining the AS_Path length. Shorter AS_Path lengths are preferred because they indicate a more direct path to the destination.

Copyright © 2024 VERSAtile Reads. All rights reserved.
This material is protected by copyright, any infringement will be dealt with legal and punitive action.

252. C) By setting the local preference attribute

Explanation: The local preference attribute in BGP is used to influence the path selection for outbound traffic. By setting a higher local preference value for a particular route, an organization can indicate to its BGP routers that this route should be preferred over others when sending traffic outside the AS. This allows organizations to implement outbound traffic engineering and control how traffic exits their network.

253. B) No_Advertise

Explanation: The BGP community value "No_Advertise" signifies that routes should not be advertised to any external BGP (eBGP) peer. It is used to prevent the advertisement of specific routes to peers outside the autonomous system (AS) to which they belong.

254. C) The longest match

Explanation: In BGP routing path selection, the prefix length determines the longest match. When multiple routes with different prefix lengths are available for the same destination, BGP prefers the route with the longest matching prefix. This ensures that the most specific route is selected, leading to more granular routing decisions.

255. A) They are preferred over shorter prefixes

Explanation:

In BGP path selection, routes with longer matching prefixes are preferred over shorter prefixes. This preference is because longer prefixes provide more specific routing information, resulting in more accurate forwarding decisions. BGP routers prioritize routes with longer prefixes to achieve granular routing control.

256. B) Initiates a soft reset for a specific address family

Copyright © 2024 VERSAtile Reads. All rights reserved.

This material is protected by copyright, any infringement will be dealt with legal and punitive action.

Explanation: The command "clear bgp afi safi {ip-address|*} soft [in | out]" initiates a soft reset for a specific address family in BGP. This command is used to reset the BGP session for the specified address family without tearing down the entire BGP session. It allows BGP routers to refresh their routing tables and exchange routing information without disrupting connectivity.

257. A) Weight

Explanation: In the BGP best-path selection algorithm, the weight attribute is evaluated first. Weight is a Cisco-specific attribute used to influence the path selection within a single router. It is assigned locally to routes based on local configuration and is not advertised to other routers. Routes with higher weight values are preferred over routes with lower weight values.

258. B) They are not advertised by default

Explanation: By default, BGP communities are not advertised to any BGP peer in IOS and IOS XE routers. BGP communities are optional transitive attributes that can be attached to BGP routes to convey additional information or policy decisions. However, for communities to be propagated to other routers, a specific configuration is required.

259. B) As two 16-bit numbers separated by a colon

Explanation: In the new format, a BGP community is displayed as two 16-bit numbers separated by a colon. This format allows for more flexibility and extensibility compared to the older format, which uses a single 32-bit number. The first 16 bits represent the autonomous system number (ASN), and the second 16 bits represent the community value.

260. B) Local Preference

Explanation: The Local Preference attribute is used within an Autonomous System (AS) to influence the path selection process by setting a preference for routes learned from different ASes. A higher local preference value

Copyright © 2024 VERSAtile Reads. All rights reserved.

This material is protected by copyright, any infringement will be dealt with legal and punitive action.

VERSAtile Reads

indicates a more preferred path. MED, or Multi-Exit Discriminator, influences external path selection, while Weight is a Cisco-specific attribute used for local router decision-making, and AS Path is used to prevent routing loops and prefer shorter paths.

261. B) Extended communities

Explanation: Extended communities are commonly used for VPN services in BGP. Extended communities provide additional flexibility and functionality compared to standard communities. They allow the encoding of more complex information, making them suitable for specifying VPN-related attributes such as route targets, route distinguishers, and service types in BGP-based VPN implementations.

262. D) By advertising a summary prefix and a longer matching prefix

Explanation: An organization can guarantee deterministic path selection outside the organization by advertising a summary prefix and a longer matching prefix. By advertising a summary prefix, the organization ensures that traffic destined for subnets within the summary range follows a predictable path. Additionally, advertising longer matching prefixes allows the organization to influence traffic engineering decisions for specific subnets or services.

263. B) To re-advertise prefixes to the requesting router

Explanation: The route refresh capability in BGP allows a BGP speaker to request the re-advertisement of prefixes from its BGP peers without tearing down the BGP session. When a BGP router receives a route refresh request from a peer, it re-advertises all prefixes from its BGP routing table to the requesting router. This capability helps synchronize routing information between BGP peers without disrupting connectivity.

264. B) No_Advertise

Copyright © 2024 VERSAtile Reads. All rights reserved.

This material is protected by copyright, any infringement will be dealt with legal and punitive action.

Explanation: The well-known BGP community value "No_Advertise" indicates that routes should not be advertised to any eBGP peer. When a BGP route is tagged with the "No_Advertise" community, it is suppressed from being advertised to any external peers, ensuring that the route remains within the local AS.

265. C) It uses all paths for load balancing

Explanation: BGP can handle multiple paths to the same destination network by using all available paths for load balancing, provided that they meet the criteria specified in the BGP best-path selection algorithm. This allows BGP routers to distribute traffic across multiple paths, improving network performance and resilience.

266. D). Router ID (RID)

Explanation: When there is a tie in the BGP best-path algorithm, the BGP router compares the Router ID (RID) of the neighboring routers. The Router ID is a unique identifier assigned to each BGP router, typically based on the highest IP address of its active interfaces. The router with the lowest RID is preferred in the event of a tie.

267. C) Router ID (RID)

Explanation: In BGP (Border Gateway Protocol), when all other attributes (such as AS Path length, Origin code, MED, etc.) are equal for multiple paths to the same destination, the Router ID (RID) is used as a tie-breaker to determine the best path. Each BGP router has a unique Router ID, which is typically the highest IP address of any of its active interfaces.

268. B) To prevent routes from being advertised to any eBGP peer

Explanation: The purpose of the well-known BGP community "No_Export" is to prevent routes from being advertised to any external BGP (eBGP) peer. When a BGP route is tagged with the "No_Export" community, it is

Copyright © 2024 VERSAtile Reads. All rights reserved.
This material is protected by copyright, any infringement will be dealt with legal and punitive action.

suppressed from being advertised to peers outside the local autonomous system (AS), ensuring that the route remains within the confines of the AS.

269. A) Weight

Explanation: When the path has the lowest IGP (Interior Gateway Protocol) next hop, the weight attribute is preferred in BGP. The weight attribute is a Cisco-specific attribute used to influence the path selection within a single router. It is assigned locally to routes based on local configuration and is not advertised to other routers.

270. B) They are preferred

Explanation: Routes with higher local preference values are preferred in the BGP best-path selection process. Local preference is a BGP attribute used to indicate the preferred exit point from an autonomous system (AS) to reach a specific destination network. Routes with higher local preference values are chosen over routes with lower values when multiple paths to the same destination exist.

271. C) Routes are not advertised to any BGP peer

Explanation: The "No_Advertise" community has the effect of preventing routes from being advertised to any BGP peer, whether external (eBGP) or internal (iBGP). When a route is tagged with the "No_Advertise" community, it is suppressed from being advertised to any BGP peer, ensuring that the route remains confined within the local autonomous system (AS).

272. B) Local preference

Explanation: The local preference attribute in BGP is used to influence the path selection for outbound traffic. By assigning higher local preference values to specific routes, an organization can control which exit points are preferred for sending traffic outside the autonomous system (AS). This

Copyright © 2024 VERSAtile Reads. All rights reserved.

This material is protected by copyright, any infringement will be dealt with legal and punitive action.

allows organizations to implement outbound traffic engineering and optimize their network performance.

273. A) To influence the path chosen for inbound traffic

Explanation: The purpose of setting the MED (Multi-Exit Discriminator) attribute in BGP is to influence the path chosen for inbound traffic. MED is used to communicate to neighboring autonomous systems (AS) the preferred path for reaching a specific destination network. By setting different MED values on outbound routes, an AS can influence how traffic enters its network from neighboring ASs.

274. A) clear bgp session ip-address

Explanation: The command "clear bgp session ip-address" clears a specific BGP session without tearing it down. It removes the BGP session's state information from the router's memory, allowing the session to be reset without interrupting BGP peering. This command is useful for troubleshooting and refreshing BGP sessions without disrupting connectivity.

275. C) The path with the lowest MED

Explanation: If BGP paths have the same weight and local preference, the BGP router selects the path with the lowest Multi-Exit Discriminator (MED) value. MED is an optional non-transitive attribute used to influence the path selection process between neighboring autonomous systems (AS). A lower MED value indicates a more preferred path for inbound traffic.

276. C) show ip route bgp

Explanation: The command "show ip route bgp" is used to display the BGP routing table for a specific network prefix on a router. It shows the BGP-learned routes that are currently installed in the router's routing table. This

Copyright © 2024 VERSAtile Reads. All rights reserved.

This material is protected by copyright, any infringement will be dealt with legal and punitive action.

command helps troubleshoot BGP routing issues and verify the BGP routing information received by the router.

277. C) It prefers the route with the shortest AS_Path

Explanation: When a BGP router handles routes with the same prefix length, it prefers the route with the shortest AS_Path. The AS_Path attribute indicates the sequence of autonomous systems (AS) through which a route has traversed. By selecting the route with the shortest AS_Path, the router aims to choose the most direct path to the destination network.

278. A) It indicates the length of the path to the destination

Explanation: The AS_Path attribute in BGP indicates the length of the path to the destination network. It consists of a sequence of AS numbers through which the route has traversed. BGP routers use the AS_Path attribute to avoid routing loops and determine the shortest path to reach a specific destination.

279. B) The route is more preferred

Explanation: Setting a higher local preference for a BGP route makes the route more preferred. Local preference is a BGP attribute used to indicate the preferred exit point from an autonomous system (AS) to reach a specific destination network. Routes with higher local preference values are chosen over routes with lower values when multiple paths to the same destination exist.

280. D) MED

Explanation: The Multi-Exit Discriminator (MED) attribute can be used to modify the AS_Path length for a specific route in BGP. While the AS_Path attribute itself represents the sequence of autonomous systems (AS) through which a route has traversed, the MED attribute allows an AS to convey to neighboring ASs the preferred path for reaching a specific destination

Copyright © 2024 VERSAtile Reads. All rights reserved.

This material is protected by copyright, any infringement will be dealt with legal and punitive action.

network. By adjusting the MED value for outbound routes, an organization can influence the AS_Path length perceived by neighboring ASs, thereby affecting inbound traffic routing decisions.

281. D) By changing the MED value

Explanation: An organization can influence the path selection for inbound traffic using BGP by changing the Multi-Exit Discriminator (MED) value. The MED attribute is used to communicate to neighboring autonomous systems (AS) the preferred path for reaching a specific destination network. By adjusting the MED value on outbound routes advertised to neighboring ASs, an organization can influence inbound traffic routing decisions, potentially attracting traffic through preferred paths.

282. B) show bgp afi safi

Explanation: The command "show bgp afi safi" displays the BGP table for a specific address family. BGP (Border Gateway Protocol) operates with multiple address families, such as IPv4 unicast, IPv6 unicast, VPNv4, VPNv6, etc. This command allows network administrators to view BGP routing information specific to a particular address family, helping them troubleshoot routing issues and analyze BGP route advertisements.

283. A) RFC 1918

Explanation: RFC 1918 specifies address ranges for private networks that should not be routed on the public Internet.

284. C) 16,777,216

Explanation: The 10.0.0.0/8 network can accommodate 2^{24} (16,777,216) hosts.

285. C) 256 hosts

Copyright © 2024 VERSAtile Reads. All rights reserved.

This material is protected by copyright, any infringement will be dealt with legal and punitive action.

Explanation: The 172.16.0.0/24 network can accommodate 2^8 (256) hosts.

286. B) 65,536

Explanation: The 192.168.0.0/16 network can accommodate 2^16 (65,536) hosts.

287. C) To enable private IP networks to connect to the public Internet

Explanation: NAT allows devices on a private network to access the public Internet by translating private IP addresses to a public IP address.

288. B) Router

Explanation: NAT is typically performed by a router, which translates private IP addresses to a public IP address.

289. A) The actual private IP address assigned to a device on the inside network

Explanation: An Inside Local address is the actual private IP address assigned to a device within the inside network.

290. B) The public IP address that represents one or more inside local IP addresses

Explanation: An Inside Global address is a public IP address assigned to represent an Inside Local address(es) on the global Internet.

291. C) The IP address of an outside host as it appears to the inside network

Explanation: An Outside Local address is the IP address of an outside host as it appears to the inside network.

Copyright © 2024 VERSAtile Reads. All rights reserved.

This material is protected by copyright, any infringement will be dealt with legal and punitive action.

292. D) The public IP address assigned to a host on the outside network

Explanation: An Outside Global address is a public IP address assigned to an outside host, visible on the global Internet.

293. A) Static NAT

Explanation: Static NAT provides a one-to-one mapping between a local IP address and a global IP address.

294. B) A dynamic one-to-one mapping of a local IP address to a global IP address

Explanation: Pooled NAT dynamically assigns a global IP address from a pool to a local IP address when needed.

295. C) To provide a dynamic many-to-one mapping of many local IP addresses to one global IP address

Explanation: PAT (also known as NAT overload) maps multiple private IP addresses to a single public IP address by using different ports.

296. B) By using a unique port

Explanation: PAT uses unique port numbers to distinguish between different private IP addresses when mapping them to a single public IP address.

297. B) ip nat outside

Explanation: The command ip nat outside is used to configure an interface as an outside interface for NAT.

298. A) ip nat inside

Copyright © 2024 VERSAtile Reads. All rights reserved.
This material is protected by copyright, any infringement will be dealt with legal and punitive action.

Explanation: The command ip nat inside is used to configure an interface as an inside interface for NAT.

299. A) 1 hour

Explanation: The default timeout period for dynamic NAT translations is 1 hour.

300. C) ip nat pool

Explanation: The command ip nat pool is used to define a pool of global IP addresses for NAT.

301. A) Generic Routing Encapsulation

Explanation: GRE stands for Generic Routing Encapsulation, a tunneling protocol developed by Cisco.

302. C) To encapsulate and forward packets over an IP-based network

Explanation: GRE tunnels are used to encapsulate a wide variety of network layer protocols to be transported over an IP network.

303. A) GRE

Explanation: GRE is typically used to create VPNs by tunneling traffic.

304. C) New header information is added

Explanation: When a packet is encapsulated in a GRE tunnel, new header information is added.

305. A) De-encapsulation

Copyright © 2024 VERSAtile Reads. All rights reserved.
This material is protected by copyright, any infringement will be dealt with legal and punitive action.

VERSAtile Reads

Explanation: The process of removing GRE headers at the remote endpoint is called de-encapsulation.

306. C) Recursive routing

Explanation: Recursive routing is a common issue when a routing protocol is used on a network tunnel, where the tunnel interface is included in the routing path.

307. C) By checking routing tables

Explanation: A router detects recursive routing by checking its routing tables and identifying routes that point back to the tunnel interface.

308. A) The tunnel is brought down

Explanation: When recursive routing is detected, the tunnel is usually brought down to prevent routing loops.

309. B) Data integrity

Explanation: The IP authentication header provides data integrity and authenticity, ensuring that data has not been tampered with.

310. B) 51

Explanation: The protocol number for the IP authentication header is 51.

311. A) Encapsulating Security Payload

Explanation: ESP stands for Encapsulating Security Payload, a protocol used in IPsec for providing confidentiality, integrity, and authenticity of data.

Copyright © 2024 VERSAtile Reads. All rights reserved.
This material is protected by copyright, any infringement will be dealt with legal and punitive action.

VERSAtile Reads

312. A) Data confidentiality

Explanation: A primary feature of ESP is data confidentiality, as it encrypts the payload of the packet.

313. A) 50

Explanation: The protocol number for ESP is 50.

314. B) Tunnel mode

Explanation: Tunnel mode encrypts the entire original IP packet, which is then encapsulated with a new IP header.

315. A) Transport mode

Explanation: Transport mode only encrypts and authenticates the payload of the IP packet, leaving the original IP header intact.

316. D) 256 bits

Explanation: AES-256 uses a 256-bit key length, providing a high level of encryption security.

317. A) Data Encryption Standard

Explanation: DES stands for Data Encryption Standard, a symmetric-key algorithm for the encryption of data.

318. B) It is very weak

Explanation: DES is considered very weak by today's standards due to its short key length (56 bits), which is vulnerable to brute-force attacks.

319. A) Triple Data Encryption Standard

Copyright © 2024 VERSAtile Reads. All rights reserved.
This material is protected by copyright, any infringement will be dealt with legal and punitive action.

Explanation: 3DES stands for Triple Data Encryption Standard, which applies the DES algorithm three times to each data block.

320. C) AES

Explanation: AES (Advanced Encryption Standard) is recommended over DES and 3DES due to its stronger security and efficiency.

321. B) 160 bits

Explanation: SHA-1 produces a hash value of 160 bits in length.

322. B) Data authentication

Explanation: MD5 (Message Digest Algorithm 5) is primarily used for data authentication by generating a 128-bit hash value to verify data integrity.

323. C) SHA

Explanation: SHA (Secure Hash Algorithm) provides better protection against Man-in-the-Middle (MitM) attacks compared to MD5, particularly SHA-256 and higher versions.

324. B) Exchanging keys

Explanation: Diffie-Hellman is used for securely exchanging cryptographic keys over a public channel.

325. C) The length of the key used for a DH key exchange

Explanation: A DH group refers to the length of the key used in the Diffie-Hellman key exchange process, affecting the security strength of the key exchange.

Copyright © 2024 VERSAtile Reads. All rights reserved.
This material is protected by copyright, any infringement will be dealt with legal and punitive action. 160

326. B) Groups 14 and higher

Explanation: Cisco recommends using DH groups 14 and higher due to their stronger security.

327. B) Authenticating peers

Explanation: RSA signatures are used for authenticating peers in various security protocols, ensuring that the communicating parties are who they claim to be.

328. C) To mutually authenticate peers

Explanation: A pre-shared key in IPsec is used to mutually authenticate peers before establishing a secure connection.

329. C) By translating overlapping IP addresses

Explanation: NAT can help manage overlapping IP address spaces by translating IP addresses from one company's network to another.

330. B) It requires many configuration entries

Explanation: A major drawback of static NAT is that it requires a separate configuration entry for each mapping, making it complex to manage.

331. B) It is returned to the pool for reuse

Explanation: In pooled NAT, the global IP address is returned to the pool for reuse once the timeout period expires.

332. D) Application-Aware Routing

Explanation: Application-Aware Routing in Cisco SD-WAN dynamically selects the best path for traffic based on real-time performance metrics such as latency, jitter, and packet loss. This ensures optimal application

Copyright © 2024 VERSAtile Reads. All rights reserved.
This material is protected by copyright, any infringement will be dealt with legal and punitive action.

performance and improves user experience by routing traffic over the best available link.

333. C) Port

Explanation: In PAT, a unique port number is used by the NAT device to track return traffic to the correct private IP address.

334. A) To configure the inside interface for NAT

Explanation: The command ip nat inside is used to designate an interface as an inside interface for NAT purposes.

335. C) Defines the global pool of IP addresses for NAT

Explanation: The command ip nat pool defines a range of global IP addresses for use in NAT translations.

336. D) Dynamic NAT

Explanation: Dynamic NAT is suitable for dynamically assigning global IP addresses to local IP addresses on an as-needed basis.

337. A) Adding new header information to the packet

Explanation: GRE encapsulation involves adding new header information to the original packet for transmission over an IP network.

338. B) Encrypts the entire original packet

Explanation: IPsec tunnel mode encrypts the entire original IP packet and encapsulates it within a new IP packet.

339. D) Configures inside pooled NAT

Copyright © 2024 VERSAtile Reads. All rights reserved.

This material is protected by copyright, any infringement will be dealt with legal and punitive action.

VERSAtile Reads

Explanation: The command ip nat inside source list acl pool nat-pool-name configures inside pooled NAT, using an access control list (ACL) and a specified NAT pool.

340. A) It can cause the tunnel to go down repeatedly

Explanation: Recursive routing can cause the tunnel to go down repeatedly due to routing loops, making the tunnel unusable.

341. B) Data confidentiality

Explanation: The IPsec ESP protocol provides data confidentiality through encryption, which the authentication header does not offer.

342. C) AES

Explanation: AES supports key lengths of 128, 192, or 256 bits, making it a versatile and secure encryption algorithm.

343. B) To establish security associations (SAs)

Explanation: The main function of Internet Key Exchange (IKE) is to establish security associations (SAs) for secure communication in IPsec.

344. B) RFC 7296

Explanation: IKEv2 is specified in RFC 7296, providing improvements over the original IKE protocol.

345. B) UDP 500

Explanation: ISAKMP (Internet Security Association and Key Management Protocol) uses UDP port 500 for communication between peers.

Copyright © 2024 VERSAtile Reads. All rights reserved.

This material is protected by copyright, any infringement will be dealt with legal and punitive action. 163

VERSAtile Reads

346. D) Incompatible with IKEv1

Explanation: IKEv2 is compatible with IKEv1, but the other options (support for EAP, anti-DoS capabilities, and fewer messages for SA establishment) are true characteristics of IKEv2.

347. C) Six

Explanation: IKEv1's Main Mode during Phase 1 negotiation involves the exchange of six messages.

348. B) To establish unidirectional IPsec SAs

Explanation: In IKEv1, Phase 2 is used to establish unidirectional IPsec Security Associations (SAs) for encrypting and authenticating data traffic.

349. B) Aggressive Mode

Explanation: Aggressive Mode is faster but less secure than Main Mode, as it exposes the identities of the peers.

350. C) Greater resistance to crypto attacks

Explanation: Perfect Forward Secrecy (PFS) provides greater resistance to cryptographic attacks by ensuring that session keys are not compromised, even if the private key of the server is compromised.

Copyright © 2024 VERSAtile Reads. All rights reserved.

This material is protected by copyright, any infringement will be dealt with legal and punitive action.

VERSAtile Reads

About Our Products

Other products from VERSAtile Reads are:

Elevate Your Leadership: The 10 Must-Have Skills

Elevate Your Leadership: 8 Effective Communication Skills

Elevate Your Leadership: 10 Leadership Styles for Every Situation

300+ PMP Practice Questions Aligned with PMBOK 7, Agile Methods, and Key Process Groups – 2024

Exam-Cram Essentials Last-Minute Guide to Ace the PMP Exam - Your Express Guide featuring PMBOK® Guide

Career Mastery Blueprint - Strategies for Success in Work and Business

Memory Magic: Unraveling the Secret of Mind Mastery

The Success Equation Psychological Foundations For Accomplishment

Fairy Dust Chronicles – The Short and Sweet of Wonder

B2B Breakthrough – Proven Strategies from Real-World Case Studies

Copyright © 2024 VERSAtile Reads. All rights reserved.
This material is protected by copyright, any infringement will be dealt with legal and punitive action.

CCSP Fast Track Master: CCSP Essentials for Exam Success

 CLF-Co2: AWS Certified Cloud Practitioner: Fast Track to Exam Success

 ITIL 4 Foundation Essentials: Fast Track to Exam Success

 CCNP Security Essentials: Fast Track to Exam Success

 Certified SCRUM Master Exam Cram Essentials

 CISSP Fast Track: Master CISSP Essentials for Exam Success

 CISA Fast Track: Master CISA Essentials for Exam Success

 CISM Fast Track: Master CISM Essentials for Exam Success

 CCSP Fast Track: Master CCSP Essentials for Exam Success

 Certified SCRUM Master Exam Cram Essentials

Copyright © 2024 VERSAtile Reads. All rights reserved.

This material is protected by copyright, any infringement will be dealt with legal and punitive action.

.

www.ingramcontent.com/pod-product-compliance
Lightning Source LLC
LaVergne TN
LVHW081344050326
832903LV00024B/1301